REVELATION: THE END OF TIMES?

Hoffman Prinsloo

Cyktiq (Pty) Ltd

This book is dedicated to all the people along my journey whilst compiling this version of the book. As I received my own revelation and sound-boarded the ideas, attempts of writing my understanding at different stages of growth, the changes, the first publication, subsequent teaching to willing hearers, re-writing and again the continuous sound-boarding to family, friends and even colleagues, to my Every Nation Rosebank Connect group at the time, my Mother and many other whom I drove up the wall with my incessant searching, talking, sharing, and teaching. Each one of you who listened, who read, who asked, even those who made as if they showed an interest or made as if they listened... I wish to say thank you. Without your ears, your eyes, your physical presence and most of all your mountains of patience, endurance and longsuffering with me, I would not have been able to come up with this version of the book. Thank you for helping me.

CONTENTS

ACKNOWLEDGMENTS

JH Africa for the cover design
Lisa Turnbull for her first edition editing assistance
Anna Elizabeth who always knew that God
through the Holy Spirit was downloading
this information and kept encouraging me
– you are to me like Mary was to Jesus

1 INTRODUCTION

I have learnt through my attempts of writing books that as we press into a subject area and also as we grow spiritually, God is faithful and rewards our efforts with growth in knowledge, wisdom and understanding. With faithful I mean, that He when we press in keeps giving us revelation into the area where we are searching. I suppose as we grow up spiritually and pursue a certain subject area, it is like digging for treasure in a mountain. The more we dig, the more we find, and the more we find the more we are inclined to press in even further until we excavate the "motherload"... if there is ever such an end to it. I hope this version of "Revelation the end of times?" is rich enough and deep enough in order for you, the reader or listener, to really enrich your own understanding and most of all bless you tremendously.

The book of Revelation, or any of the revelation scriptures for that matter is probably some of the most un-read or even mis-understood pieces of literature, do you not think and also experience that? I really struggled with it. From my first attempts of reading the book of Revelation in the Bible, to my first attempt of jotting down notes, to searching the internet for videos and literature, to reading books on it, to my first publishing attempt, I really found it quite complex to lay out and understand. Sometimes I would have a moment of light and understanding, but then some other scripture or someone else's take on it would confuse me and send me scuttling back to the drawing board.

From my own experience I think it is important and we should take a few key points into any attempt when we personally handle the Revelation scriptures. These include some of the thoughts that follow. Yes, we should be concerned about the times we are living in. But at the same time we should also clearly see God's grace and mercy in it. If we at any time miss God's heart when we listen to, read or study Revelation or end time words of wisdom preached by people we should stop and first find God the Father's heart in the midst of it. What do I mean with that... Simply this, that irrespective of the fear mongering, the events, even the wrath... God the Father remains love, patience, endurance, long-suffering, goodness, peace, humility and does not parade Himself. He keeps on caring for the widows, the parentless children, the stranger, the broken and the down trodden. Anyone with a broken spirit and contrite heart remains His prime area of interest. Turning souls to Him, healing hearts, renewing the way we think of Him and who we are to Him will always remain the most pressing matter on God's heart – irrespective the crisis, the disaster, the hatred, the brokenness that we encounter. And we are called to minister to people's souls, hearts, minds and bodies first and foremost and touch their emotions, feelings and thoughts and turn their ears and eyes to the wonder of His love for them. If we forget that in our end times escotology, end times prophecy and words of wisdom, then God is not in it.

We should also clearly distinguish the where, when and what in the sequence of events that we are considering. If we do not place an event in the right sequence or misplace an event we will walk away more confused than when we commenced engaging with it. I personally found that the amount of nonsense, false teaching, obsession with end times prophecy, and fear mongering is all distractions into really finding the truth and the blessing and the preparation required for the events to come.

There are two very important aspects to take note of before you even commence to engage with this book. The first is some truth that Dr David Pawson said in a video that I happened to peruse. He said that there are only two kinds of people when it comes to the book of Revelation. Firstly there are those who never get into the book of Revelation, and secondly there are those who never get out of the book of Revelation. And I think both are equally as unfortunate as the other. Revelation is given to us to prepare ourselves, but also to greatly bless us knowing that God our Father is always in control and His mercy is evidenced throughout. But people constantly in the book of Revelation miss the point that there is near six thousand years of Christ history on the earth, and whether you stand at the beginning of that history, in the middle of it, or at the end, it all points to a loving Father full of mercy and a Saviour full of grace. And we should study it all, and admire it all in order to catch the heart of God and His purpose for us. And we need all of it to live rich lives in community with our brothers and sisters in this age. Therefore I would recommend that you get into Revelation and immerse yourself in it, but then get out of it again and focus on God's heart, and then repeat this cycle to get an even fuller revelation of it.

The second very important aspect that I have learnt myself and something that I eluded to earlier is that Revelation will grow on you and open up for you as you press on. My experience of writing on any subject on matters related to the Kingdom of God is that it keeps getting richer, deeper and keeps opening up as you work with it. My experience is much like when I was a young boy. My mother was an artist and used to paint oil paintings. She was and still is a very gifted and a creative painter. Probably because she was always a godly woman and therefore having a touch of God's creativity in her. But if it was up to her she would never-ever finish a painting. I have seen her sell many paintings, and then when we happened to visit the person she sold the painting to she would actually take her brush and touch-up the painting hanging in the person's home or office! The worst I ever experienced was when she did a wall mural on an entire section of wall in my father's snooker room.

It was initially a massive depiction of Gemsbok at a water-hole in Namibia in the shimmering heat. It was beautiful and a real master piece. But, she then painted an entire new scene over the poor Gemsbok. And so it went on for years. I still think one day some new owner of our childhood home will be able to sell that wall for a fortune, with layer after layer of master paintings one on top of the other. It is exactly the same with me and this Revelation book that you are about to engage with. By the time I am finished with the last page, I will already have received a whole wealth of richness from God my Father to start re-writing the entire book again. Hopefully one day we can rather meet, and I can give you a fuller impartation of what I have come to understand in the interim – than to continue updating this book or version.

The first published version of my book Revelation the End of Times was not my best effort when I now look back at it. The hardcopy of that first version is still available on Amazon, and for some reason I cannot update or delete it. It is like a memorial set up in time. There is quite a bit of truth in it though, I would say 70% of it is quite strong in truth. However in my opinion it does not reflect a good effort now that I am a few years older and spiritually more mature as a Christian. Since that publication I received more in depth understanding on the subject. However, some of the events such as for example fires consuming entire areas was just about non-existent in 2015 when I first published. When I wrote back then I searched wide on the topic but found very little occurrence of it back then. Now in 2024 and 2025 wide ranging fires in nature has found its common place in society and in the news. Everywhere you look and read you see massive natural disasters of fire ranging from California, to the Amazon, Spain, Australia, China, South Africa etc. This book will not focus inasmuch on that which I wrote back then. If you could however compare that book with this version, you will note that the content has become much richer. There were things back then which I could simply not see at all, with a very important emphasis on the word see (the word see, or eyes which can see, which I will clarify as we continue in this study of ours). If you are more mature than me as a Christian when you read this book you will probably be able to say that my insight is perhaps a bit shallow-ish. Much like an older sibling thinking their little brother has little experience of this life. But, if I am more mature than you spiritually you will find the work quite rich. But one thing is for sure, that if I continue to press into God my Father through our Lord Jesus Christ morning after morning in the secret place even I will think this book needs updating in a year from now. And that is the second point - engage with this book, and then get into and then out of the book of Revelation yourself. And then the next time you yourself engage with it, it will be much richer for you also.

2 THE MESSENGER

I n my first edition of the book Revelation the End of Times, I introduced myself as if to introduce myself to the reading community. And I do not want that to be the focus of this chapter this time. Rather this time I want us to focus on the author of the book Revelation, namely John. I think there are very important spiritual principles that we need to learn of this man and how he came about to be the author of Revelation, in order for us to grasp his message. Hopefully that will give us some good insights into our own salvation journey.

We meet John for the first time in the Gospels and also in his own witness version in the book John. Jesus calls John as one of the inner circle of twelve disciples whilst John was busy fishing by the sea of Galilee with his father Zebedee. Jesus not only calls John but also his brother James. Can you just imagine what a privilege it was for John and his brother James to have witnessed Jesus first-hand for many years. The family conversations between two brothers, after Jesus ascended into heaven, must surely have grown their faith or at least their encouragement towards one another, don't you think? One could perhaps even argue then that the purposeful calling of the two brothers were intentional. Especially if we consider that the first two disciples called were also bothers namely Peter and Andrew, and how Peter became the lead influencer for the early Jewish Christian church. Perhaps this pairing of brothers gave them so much more depth during and after their accounts with Jesus, we could muse?

It is not the intention to get too technical here, and not so soon in this book. But if we think about the three main Jewish festivals from the Old Testament you will note that the Passover (accompanied by the feast of unleavened bread), the feast of Weeks (or Pentecost as we celebrate it today), and lastly the feast of Tabernacles were the three main festivals that God said would be kept in perpetuity, or in eternity. We will always commemorate the major events that has and that will take place during these days. I want us to make a note here that Jesus commenced His ministry on the feast of Tabernacles when he went into the synagogue and read from the book of Isaiah and after He closed it said: "Today, this scripture is fulfilled". And three and a half years later Jesus was crucified, died and was resurrected on the feast of Passover. Although not clearly depicted in scripture, we can bet our bottom dollar, John the Baptist also had a ministry of three and a half years commencing on the Feast of Passover and three and a half years later ended ultimately leading to his decapitation. This would give us a perfect prophetic cycle of seven years, broken into two three and a half year cycles. Remember this three and a half year cycle followed by another three and a half year cycle for the perfect prophetic cycle when the Kingdom of God again draws near in the book of Revelation. When we revisit this type of a cycle later in Revelation it will sound familiar to you. I want you also to make a note here for yourself that the feast of Tabernacles is the only unfulfilled prophetic feast that we have today. And again, we can make a note to ourselves that Jesus will return for His second coming as the Christ on this largest of all the festivals to be celebrated in perpetuity.

I wanted to highlight this three and a half year cycle, including the notes you made to yourself as requested above. Because from the time Jesus Christ commenced His ministry on the feast of Tabernacles until it ended on the feast of Passover something amazing happened to John under Jesus' discipleship - his "eyes" were opened. I specifically highlighted the word eyes because it means eyes in the spiritual sense. After John spent three and a half years with Jesus, John's eyes was the only pair of all the disciples that was opened by the time Jesus was ready to ascend to heaven. You might argue with me and say it is not so, or how can you be so sure you might ask? And in childlike faith I will tell you that it is so because scripture or eye witness account tells us so. Let us consider in John's own eye witness account what transpired on that day that the disciples realised it. Before we do that, please make a note to yourself that our discipleship journey commences with the redemption of our souls, followed by the redemption of our hearts, then the redemption of our minds and most importantly is followed by the opening of our ears to hear and then our eyes to see. And these seeing eyes is where our revelations come from. It is not the purpose to go into all of that here and if you want real meat on this processes I beseech you to read *Christian unity: Walking in a motivating climate by Hoffman Prinsloo* and *You are what you eat by Hoffman Prinsloo*. This account for the corporate's and the individual's growth respectively will assist you greatly in your understanding.

But as for John we see in John's account of the breakfast by the sea how it was only John's eyes that were opened by that time. In other words John was spiritually the most mature of the remainder of eleven disciples after three and a half years of discipleship under Jesus. The scene described in John 21 describes how Jesus stood in His post-resurrection form on the shore. We cannot exactly comprehend this, because it is already something quite spiritual in its purity. And to recognize Him in this form you need spiritual eyes that can see. And John had them. We account how seven of the disciples are making their way to the shore where Jesus is standing. Jesus made a fire to cook breakfast on, and was now standing on the beach waiting for the seven men that went out fishing to return with fish. As the seven disciples draw nearer to shore they observe this man standing there by the fire. But only one can see him. Only one man's eyes are spiritually trained to recognize him – and that is the eyes of John. Now also note that the person second closest to John in spiritual growth is Peter. Peter's spiritual ears are open at this time, but he still cannot see and need to grow a little further. And the remainder of the disciples follow, as it should be. In other words in spiritual terms, we should always allow the Saint with spiritual open eyes to tell us what they see. You could say in church terms that would be the apostolic leaders. Then those with open ears should hear them in order to act and tell the others. And then finally the rest of the disciples should follow the lead of those with open eyes and ears until they themselves come to spiritual maturity to see and hear also. Now account in the scripture below how John's eyes were the only pair that could see on this day:

*"After these things **Jesus showed Himself again to the disciples** at the Sea of Tiberias, and in this way He showed Himself: Simon Peter, Thomas called the Twin, Nathanael of Cana in Galilee, the sons of Zebedee, and two others of His disciples were together. Simon Peter said to them, "I am going fishing." They said to him, "We are going with you also." They went out and immediately got into the boat, and that night they caught nothing. But when the morning had now come, Jesus stood on the shore; **yet the disciples did not know that it was Jesus**. Then Jesus said to them, "Children, have you any food?" They answered Him, "No." And He said to them, "Cast the net on the right side of the boat, and you will find some." So they cast, and now they were not able to draw it in because of the multitude of fish. Therefore **that disciple whom Jesus loved said to Peter, "It is the Lord!"** Now **when Simon Peter heard that it was the Lord**, he put on his outer garment (for he had removed it), and plunged into the sea. But the **other disciples came in the little boat** (for they were not far from land, but about two hundred cubits), dragging the net with fish. Then, as soon as they had come to land, they saw a fire of coals there, and fish laid on it, and bread. Jesus said to them, "Bring some of the fish which you have just caught.""* John 21:1 - 10 NKJV

Interesting isn't it, when you look at it this way? There were these disciples, all after three and a half years under discipleship of Jesus the Christ and only John can see at this stage. John many times calls himself the disciple whom Jesus loved in the book of John. Now, we might argue today that John was quite full of himself to say that. But from early Christian church accounts when John was an old man he was anything but vain. Then if not vanity what else could John mean and why would he often say "that disciple whom Jesus loved" when he accounts of himself. What John is referring to is his spiritual maturity. John is not talking about religious knowledge but spiritual maturity or growth. Yes, we know today that John must have been in the inner-circle in the religious circle of the Temple and especially with him knowing and similarly the family of the high priest knowing John and his family. That is evidently why John could slip into the hearing of Jesus before the high priest, and why we have eye witness account of what was said during this closed hearing. No, it is not this maturity as a Jewish scholar that John is talking about. John is talking about himself in reference to the growth phases of spiritual maturity that he himself references in 1 John 2: 12 – 14. Firstly we repent, believe in Jesus Christ, are baptised into Jesus Christ through water, and receive the Holy Spirt for the redemption of our soul. That is the infant or "little children" phase. We then grow in heart to heart relationship with the Father by spending morning by morning time with Him in the secret place. That is the "young men" phase. Then through trials and tribulation, in a baptism of fire if you like, or during a wilderness walk, or a crucible experience where some of our riches including relationships, finances and health are taken away from us we mature. That is the "father" phase if you like. This phase of growth is described by the apostle Paul as where through trials and tribulation we learn to persevere in order for our character to build, until we walk into the hope of our promise. And what is this promise you might ask? Our ears are opened to hear and our eyes are opened to see. Or in the words of David after all his riches, including close relationships, finances and health were taken from him he said – "if only I can wake this morning with eyes to see You, ears to hear you and my heart to know You God". That is spiritual maturity, when we have learnt through experience to stand in rest, quietness and confidence in the presence of God our Father irrespective our circumstances. Let us consider John's description of this growth path that he must have known intimately in order to have penned it:

*"I write to you, **little children**, Because your sins are forgiven you for His name's sake. I write to you, **fathers**, Because you have known Him who is from the beginning. I write to you, **young men**, Because you have overcome the wicked one. I write to you, **little children**, Because you have known the Father. I have written to you, **fathers**, Because you have known Him who is from the beginning. I have written to you, **young men**, Because you are strong, and the word of God abides in you, And you have overcome the wicked one."*

I John 2:12-14 NKJV

What we are talking about here is the call to perfection. Now, in my own experience when the word perfection is used the Saints have a near violent reaction to its use. We are easy to mis-use the word salvation. We often hear that a person is said to be salvaged when he first announces with his mouth that he accepts Jesus and to from there believe in Jesus Christ. The person has scarcely commenced on his journey of a salvation walk and process and already we declare – "he is salvaged". But when we say a person's spiritual eyes are opened to see and spiritual ears are opened to hear declaring – "he is perfected", we tend to violently defend that that is not a possible state for a Saint to reach. Allow me to walk you slowly through our discipleship growth phases. We commence with the redemption of our souls (little children phase), followed by the redemption of our hearts (young men phase), followed by the redemption of our minds (father phase) to perfection (the opening of our eyes to see and our ears to hear) and then finally onto salvation when Jesus Christ returns with our final growth aspect – a new body or vessel to contain all of the previous gains.

And that is why John was the one disciple that could write the book of Revelation. John was spiritually the most mature of them all. How he did it or managed to grow quicker than anyone else is as good a guess of yours as it is mine. We can just meditate on it and guess that it has much to do with John's propensity for relationship with Jesus Christ and God the Father. In other words John had a heart inclined to relationship. You can imagine some of this relationship if you contemplate how he was the one with his head closest to Jesus' chest when they shared the last supper – always within an ear's distance from Jesus. Or how his Revelation writing style was more in the form of a campfire story. John did not write like Paul did in a Greek-style of linear form. John wrote in circles like you would tell a story, more focussed on warming the relationship than getting the facts across like the apostle Paul would. And I suspect that is why John accelerated in his spiritual growth under Jesus Christ – because John was more focussed on relationship as opposed to religious facts.

And that is our messenger of the book of Revelation – John the spiritually mature disciple whose eyes were opened first of all the inner-disciples to Jesus and who was relationship focussed.

3 THE WOMAN

The theme or rather the image of the woman is very strong in any of the Bible prophecies, including in that of Revelation. But especially in the book of Revelation this theme of the woman becomes quite descriptive and the actions of the woman described in more colour and detail than many of the older Old Testament prophecies. The purpose of this chapter then is to delve a little deeper into this picture of the woman in the book of Revelation.

Note in Revelation 12 that there is a great sign, or a star sign, in the heavens that describes a woman. Now in order to understand this picture of the woman, we should assume for a moment that the history forming the picture of Christ, from the first time we meet Adam and Eve in the book of Genesis up to the second coming of Jesus Christ is approximately 6 000 years. In fact if you refer to the Jewish calendar website www.hebcal.com we are living in the year 5 785 from the commencement of this history. Your first thought might be, as mine was, that if we have to wait until the 6 000 there is still 215 years ahead – phew! But be careful, because if you look into the book of Daniel you will note that the last days or weeks will be substantially shortened, otherwise the World itself wouldn't make it… never mind you or me. We might therefore just be surprised – with a proverbial suddenly! On this 5 782 timeline Jesus was born in the year 3 760 from the time we get to know of Adam in the garden of Eden. And we can guess that on this continuous timeline Jesus was crucified and ascended into Heaven more or less in the year 3 794 during His 34th year on the Earth. If we can imagine that from the year 1 to the year 3 794 we can talk about "men being born of woman" and from the year 3 794 to the present year 5 785 and onward we can talk about the dispensation of "men being born of Spirit". To place this into Biblical context we can recall that Jesus Himself referred to John the Baptist as the greatest of all the prophets "born of woman" but that the least of the saints born after John that is "born of Spirit" is greater than John the Baptist. This description of this history from the year 1 to the year 3 794 encompassing people such as Adam, Noah, Abraham, Isaac, Jacob, David, Israel and Judah all help to form the picture of the head of this woman and her body in the process and up to where the Christ is born – namely Jesus and His ascension into Heaven. For this period prior to Jesus' birth, His sacrifice and His ascension into heaven we can see "men being born of woman" or in the "natural". But then with Jesus as the first man being born in the Spirit and more specifically raised from death by the Spirit we see a new era starting of men now being "born of Spirit" of which Jesus Christ was the "first fruit". From this day of the "first fruit" the history of the Church, up to our present time, then forms the picture of the legs and the feet of the woman and every "birth of a man of Spirit" during this Church dispensation is "fruit" of the woman. The woman is therefore a spiritual picture of the Spiritual history on how Jesus as the Christ (meaning the son of God) came to be born, and thereafter every spiritual birth of a Saint birthed into the Kingdom of God through Christ in the Spirit. If you meditate on this picture of the woman as you read Old Testament texts or New Testament texts you will start seeing how this picture forms and this woman comes to life. In Revelation 12, we finally see the woman in a very specific role of giving birth to a "male child". This points to a ripeness in time where the woman is finally ready to birth a "male child", consisting of 144 000 young men, that will ultimately return to rule with Jesus Christ during His millennial rule with an iron sceptre:

"Now a great sign appeared in heaven: a woman clothed with the sun, with the moon under her feet, and on her head a garland of twelve stars. Then being with child, she cried out in labor and in pain to give birth." Revelation 12:1 - 2 NKJV

It is extremely important that we note for ourselves that this Woman represents the sanctuary of God on the Earth. God has a sanctuary in Heaven which we can study in the book of Hebrews 8: 1 to 6. The Woman is the representative of this heavenly sanctuary and administers or is responsible to disciple true believers from infancy to perfection in accordance to the image given her of the sanctuary in Heaven. Therefore we should note to ourselves here that the image of a woman represents a copy or a shadow or the pattern of the heavenly sanctuary and accompanying ministry.

The other repetitive theme than that of the woman we should note, especially visible in Revelation, is that there is a sequence of events. We first see the woman, knowing now that it encompasses the history and sanctuary on earth of how Christians come to be born for a spiritual Kingdom. Then we see a description of a beast or dragon on which the woman rides, with this beast depicting a kingdom. And from the result of this woman sitting on the kingdom beast if you prefer, them knowing or having communion with each other, spiritual mature men and woman are born. Then the children or offspring's actions or deeds participate in the formation of a city. In the case of a pure woman sitting on the Kingdom of God we see that the actions of the off-spring form or cover a city, namely the new Jerusalem. And conversely we see late in Revelation the picture of a harlot woman sitting on an earthly kingdom whose off-spring lead to the formation of a city, in such a case Babylon. There is therefore in the book of Revelation a contrasting picture painted of two kingdoms, two sanctuaries, two sets of off-spring leading to the formation of two contrasting cities. You could reason that in the book of Revelation John does not paint the picture of the positive process consisting of the pure woman (as seen in Revelation 12), riding on the Kingdom of God. A Kingdom with processes including how systems such as economy, a war machine, money, laws, relationships and so forth function from which the city Jerusalem is formed. Remember when John writes Revelation he writes it from the perspective of standing in the Spiritual Kingdom of God and how material events are seen through Heaven's eyes. John was too good a story teller to sketch both positive and negative versions of the same spiritual picture, and that he knew that the positive picture would and could be formed in the imagination of the Saint through own meditation and relating to Old Testament texts. John however goes to great lengths to describe the anti-type or negative portrait in the penning of Revelation. He paints a picture of how the scarlet woman (or you could reason a prostitute) rides on the beast from the sea (the anti-type of the Kingdom of God namely a kingdom formed by men's interpretation of economy, war machine, money, laws, relationships etc.). From this communion between the beast and the impure woman, or we could reason sanctuary, men and woman are born from whose actions the city Babylon is formed. It is very important that you burn this picture into your mind. We are going to go out on a limb early on with a hypothesis that it is a description that from the same definition of Church two cultures – one in the Spirit and one in the flesh - people or end destinations or cities are born, the one destined for heaven and the other for hell. Then as you read throughout the remainder of this book, and in future Scripture reading that the entire Revelation painting describes the Church (or two woman that should embody the sanctuary in heaven and its ministry) and the two kinds of people that will be produced from it. Based on this premise the vision of Revelation represents a picture that the entire battle is for the territory of the people in the Church and what those people represent. We then leave it up to each individual reader to contemplate and meditate on the weight of this hypothesis as we proceed. Let's leave it there and proceed.

But remember our early assumption as we look into Revelation: that it describes the events that have bearing on the territory of the Church represented by two Woman, depending on the kingdom she fornicates with, end up producing two kinds of churched people, one group being goats destined for hell and one ecclesia being sheep destined for heaven.

The theme of the woman is a repetitive theme and more or less describes the woman in three settings, but with the same purpose. As we contemplated earlier the picture of the woman represents the sanctuary of God the Father here on the earth... or a replica or representation of the true sanctuary of God in heaven. We first encounter the woman in the story of Adam and Eve. We then see the woman in the story of Israel. We could say that the story of two sanctuaries or two woman (Oholah and Oholibah) representing the nation Israel in Samaria and the nation Judah in Jerusalem is a third (self-study Ezekiel 23), but to keep it short we will treat Israel as a unified Nation and then the later occurrence of Israel as a Nation and Judah as a Nation as one occurrence. And finally we see the woman in the story of Revelation. Eve, Israel and the Church represent an increasing build-up or Revelation of what God intended or the romance He intended. Let's delve a little deeper into this story in order for us to pick-up on the patterns.

In the history of Adam and Eve we see the description of a pure husband and a pure wife that is placed in the garden of Eden. Now, there are a few things we should note here. Adam and Eve only knew good and did not know or had knowledge of evil at all. We do not need to go into too much description here, but if you struggle to comprehend the picture of it, please try and read *"You are what you eat"* by *Hoffman Prinsloo*, that will give you an in depth feeling for the picture and description that follows:

GOD = Good
- love
- wise
- righteous
- upright
- just

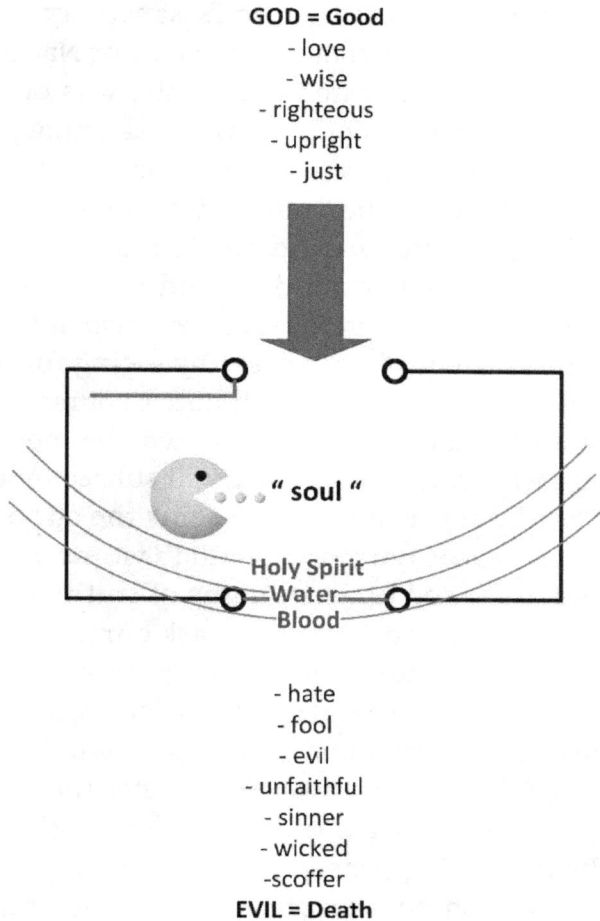

" soul "

Holy Spirit
Water
Blood

- hate
- fool
- evil
- unfaithful
- sinner
- wicked
-scoffer
EVIL = Death

The picture depicts our soul chamber that has a bottom door, that is closed to evil. And a top door that is open to good. Only one door can be open at a time, and in the case of Adam and Eve the bottom door has never been opened. The Pac Man represents the soul, and in the case of Adam and Eve it only ever learned to chomp on good wholesome spiritual food with the top door open. That is until the pure woman stepped out of her God ordained responsibility to honour God and her husband as her Spiritual authority. In the case of Adam and Eve, Eve's deception came about by not referring Satan's deceitful offer to eat of the fruit from their Tree of Good and Evil through

Adam to God. She represented God's sanctuary in Eden and was instructed not to eat that specific tree or Nation's fruit. In fact what is not said or stated is that she was on the inverse mandated to accurately represent God's sanctuary in heaven, and on the contrary she was responsible to offer fruit from and in-graft others onto the Tree of Life. The acceptance of the spiritually deceitful offer was Adam's to make, never Eve's. Eve is deceived, opens the bottom door and falls in sin. She then offers the same deceitful promise to her husband, and he does not stand but falls with her into sin by eating forbidden fruit. Actually as a short insert we should note to ourselves that once the representative sanctuary is corrupted the men ministered or discipled through that sanctuary will subsequently also fall. When Eve as his helper falls and presents the alternate fruit to Adam he himself does not stand on God's words but falls on his own interpretation and understanding of truth. And the rest is history. But what we should actually ask ourselves is what was Adam and Eve's mandate? Well, it was quite simple. They were placed in the centre of the garden of Eden into the middle of a bigger surrounding area and population. And from this pure environment, Adam and Eve was to influence their surrounding area and people by being a true reflection of the children of God. But the inverse happened and Adam and Eve allowed their surrounding environment to lure them into corruption.

This picture of the woman repeats itself for a second time and this time in a much larger environment. The nation of Israel is hand selected by God in Egypt, to turn away from Egypt (in other words repentance of sin through blood), taken through the parted Red Sea (in other words baptism in water) and appear before God in front of the fiery mountain Sinai (in other words baptism in the Holy Spirit). Then from there they are taken through a wilderness walk and experience until their culture is such that they fairly represent God's people when they enter and are gifted the promised land. And their mandate we might ask? Well with the sanctuary Zion, the woman, in the city Jerusalem their mandate was the same as that of Adam and Eve to represent God and disciple citizens from Israel and from the nations that immediately surround them. But again from prophetic description we see that Israel failed in this mandate and conversely allows their neighbours to influence them by adopting the surrounding Nation's spiritual religions and customs. Carefully read through the very emotive and descriptive prophetic words of Ezekiel for Israel, which should give us a feeling for Israel's failure in their mandate:

"and say, 'Thus says the Lord God to Jerusalem: "Your birth and your nativity are from the land of Canaan; your father was an Amorite and your mother a Hittite. As for your nativity, on the day you were born your navel cord was not cut, nor were you washed in water to cleanse you; you were not rubbed with salt nor wrapped in swaddling cloths. No eye pitied you, to do any of these things for you, to have compassion on you; but you were thrown out into the open field, when you yourself were loathed on the day you were born. "And when I passed by you and saw you struggling in your own blood, I said to you in your blood, 'Live!' Yes, I said to you in your blood, 'Live!' I made you thrive like a plant in the field; and you grew, matured, and became very beautiful. Your breasts were formed, your hair grew, but you were naked and bare. "When I passed by you again and looked upon you, indeed your time was the time of love; so I spread My wing over you and covered your nakedness. Yes, I swore an oath to you and entered into a covenant with you, and you became Mine," says the Lord God. "Then I washed you in water; yes, I thoroughly washed off your blood, and I anointed you with oil. I clothed you in embroidered cloth and gave you sandals of badger skin; I clothed you with fine linen and covered you with silk. I adorned you with ornaments, put bracelets on your wrists, and a chain on your neck. And I put a jewel in your nose, earrings in your ears, and a beautiful crown on your head. Thus you were adorned with gold and silver, and your clothing was of fine linen, silk, and embroidered cloth. You ate pastry of fine flour, honey, and oil. You were exceedingly beautiful, and succeeded to royalty. Your fame went out among the nations because of your beauty, for it was perfect through My splendor which I had bestowed on you," says the

Lord God. "But you trusted in your own beauty, played the harlot because of your fame, and poured out your harlotry on everyone passing by who would have it. You took some of your garments and adorned multicolored high places for yourself, and played the harlot on them. Such things should not happen, nor be. You have also taken your beautiful jewelry from My gold and My silver, which I had given you, and made for yourself male images and played the harlot with them. You took your embroidered garments and covered them, and you set My oil and My incense before them. Also My food which I gave you—the pastry of fine flour, oil, and honey which I fed you— you set it before them as sweet incense; and so it was," says the Lord God. "Moreover you took your sons and your daughters, whom you bore to Me, and these you sacrificed to them to be devoured. Were your acts of harlotry a small matter, that you have slain My children and offered them up to them by causing them to pass through the fire? And in all your abominations and acts of harlotry you did not remember the days of your youth, when you were naked and bare, struggling in your blood. "Then it was so, after all your wickedness —'Woe, woe to you!' says the Lord God— that you also built for yourself a shrine, and made a high place for yourself in every street. You built your high places at the head of every road, and made your beauty to be abhorred. You offered yourself to everyone who passed by, and multiplied your acts of harlotry. You also committed harlotry with the Egyptians, your very fleshly neighbors, and increased your acts of harlotry to provoke Me to anger. "How degenerate is your heart!" says the Lord God, "seeing you do all these things, the deeds of a brazen harlot. "You erected your shrine at the head of every road, and built your high place in every street. Yet you were not like a harlot, because you scorned payment. You are an adulterous wife, who takes strangers instead of her husband. Men make payment to all harlots, but you made your payments to all your lovers, and hired them to come to you from all around for your harlotry. You are the opposite of other women in your harlotry, because no one solicited you to be a harlot. In that you gave payment but no payment was given you, therefore you are the opposite.""
Ezekiel 16:3-26, 30-34 NKJV

It should then come as no surprise to us that the final stage for the woman is set where the Church, the woman, is now placed globally in every language, tongue and nation. And the mandate of the Church we might ask? The mandate of the Church is to represent God's sanctuary accurately and to minister to and disciple congregants to be in-grafted as Spiritual babies and grown to perfected saints or Christians inheriting a heavenly Kingdom and change to the heavenly culture. But not to our surprise, again it seems that the world around the Church is influencing the Church and the Church not birthing children in the Holy Spirit and growing Christians to yield edible fruit to their surroundings and leaves to heal their representative Nation.

If we can wrap our heads around the following images our ability to grasp the picture painted in Revelation will increase exponentially. In the first scene Eve represented the sanctuary of God on the earth. Her task was to fairly represent the process by which an individual is in-grafted into the Tree-of Life and matured to the point of bearing fruit and leaves. In the second scene the Temple in Zion represented the woman in Jerusalem, by which individuals from surrounding Nations could become in-grafted into the Kindgom of God. And in the final scene the Church is the sanctuary or woman responsible to convert, oversee and mature the individual Christian to bear Spiritual fruit. We should be wide awake with the following statement: the individual congregant should bear Spiritual fruit... not the Church, its shepherds or leadership. We should let go of this notion that the Church is the Woman Jesus Christ marries... the New Jerusalem is. The Church ultimately disappears as sanctuary just as Eve did and the Temple in Jerusalem did. It is the fruit of the individual Christian's actions and service that forms the covering of the new City Jerusalem that is given as wife or present to Jesus Christ. And the representative sanctuary on earth or the Church disappears in the final dispensation when God Himself comes to live amongst us. If the Church proverbially eats of the idols of the Nations, or the Church mis-understands or oversteps its mandate to grow mature sons and daughters that serve diligently she becomes prostitute like in its spiritual representation.

The question now is will the Church fulfil its mandate? And the answer is mixed at best. Yes and no. It is quite evident from Jesus Christ's parables and from the book of Revelation itself that the Apostle John himself was quite surprised when he is shown a scarlet woman, riding on a kingdom beast that is not the Kingdom of God but of men. Consequently it seems from this scarlet woman in the book of Revelation riding on the beast that the mandate for the Church is then also lost, as it were for Eve and Israel. Or is the mandate not entirely lost we might ask? We might think that the mandate is lost at first glance... but, that is where the book of Revelation starts speaking hope into us. Although it might by current world standards seem as if the Church is fighting a losing battle and the scarlet woman description in Revelation similarly paint a bleak picture – but God's mercy is not to be outdone. Our good Father seems to have a few mercy tricks up His sleeve, and we read of them in the book of Revelation. Because in Revelation we see the Husband eventually receive His bride from His Father for a traditional wedding ceremony, not unlike that of the Jewish culture in the old testament. It is a romantic love story with a happy ending. But before we get there, there are numerous last minute events to showcase God's mercy, quite a bit of deceit at attempting to deceive, and then only the prophesied gift of the New Jerusalem as bride to the Groom.

We can end this Chapter with a silent contemplation whether there is Scriptural president that the woman or sanctuary or church and especially the actions of their shepherds or leaders lead to the pain and suffering of her individual congregants. In our contemplation of this and God's heartfelt pain and subsequent fiery actions towards the sanctuary and its shepherds in the prophetic words of Ezekiel start colouring our painting of Revelation:

"And the word of the Lord came to me, saying, "Son of man,

*prophesy against the shepherds of Israel, prophesy and say to them,
'Thus says the Lord God to the shepherds: "Woe to the shepherds
of Israel who feed themselves! Should not the shepherds feed the
flocks? You eat the fat and clothe yourselves with the wool; you
slaughter the fatlings, but you do not feed the flock. The weak you
have not strengthened, nor have you healed those who were sick,
nor bound up the broken, nor brought back what was driven away,
nor sought what was lost; but with force and cruelty you have
ruled them. So they were scattered because there was no shepherd;
and they became food for all the beasts of the field when they were
scattered. My sheep wandered through all the mountains, and on
every high hill; yes, My flock was scattered over the whole face of the
earth, and no one was seeking or searching for them." 'Therefore,
you shepherds, hear the word of the Lord: "As I live," says the Lord
God, "surely because My flock became a prey, and My flock became
food for every beast of the field, because there was no shepherd,
nor did My shepherds search for My flock, but the shepherds fed
themselves and did not feed My flock"— therefore, O shepherds,
hear the word of the Lord! Thus says the Lord God: "Behold, I am
against the shepherds, and I will require My flock at their hand;
I will cause them to cease feeding the sheep, and the shepherds
shall feed themselves no more; for I will deliver My flock from their
mouths, that they may no longer be food for them."* Ezekiel 34:1-10

In Revelation we will note that there are two woman, one pure and one described as a harlot. Understanding that a woman can only be called a harlot if she first belonged to the Husband is crucial to grasp – he would have no business calling her pure or impure. Putting in in understandable language only a Church representing the true sanctuary of God in heaven can be called a harlot. That is if she no longer ministers according to the pattern shown us in heaven. No other ministry can therefore qualify for the use of the Revelation words harlot... unless it purports to represent an image of the true sanctuary and ministry in Heaven.

4 THE FIELD

"And from the time that the daily sacrifice is taken away, and the abomination of desolation is set up, there shall be one thousand two hundred and ninety days. Blessed is he who waits, and comes to the one thousand three hundred and thirty-five days." - Daniel

After considering the picture of the woman, we should realize that there is repetition in the picture of Eden and Eve, the Promised Land and Israel and the area of the Church and the Christians. And we can learn lessons from the one in order to colour our picture of the other. They all paint the same picture. And so does the picture of the field, or the vineyard, that is vividly described by the Old Testament prophet Isaiah. We should then also not be surprised that this picture of the field and the events in it was repetitive themes used in Old Testament and New Testament language. There were great and overlapping similarities that the field was first represented by the Garden of Eden, then the Promised Land and now the Church. Carefully study the story of the field so vividly prophesied by Isaiah as a vineyard, which if you meditate on it, you can imagine Adam & Eve, then Israel and then the Church:

"Now let me sing to my Well-beloved A song of my Beloved regarding His vineyard: My Well-beloved has a vineyard On a very fruitful hill. He dug it up and cleared out its stones, And planted it with the choicest vine. He built a tower in its midst, And also made a winepress in it; So He expected it to bring forth good grapes, But it brought forth wild grapes. "And now, O inhabitants of Jerusalem and men of Judah, Judge, please, between Me and My vineyard. What more could have been done to My vineyard That I have not done in it? Why then, when I expected it to bring forth good grapes, Did it bring forth wild grapes? And now, please let Me tell you what I will do to My vineyard: I will take away its hedge, and it shall be burned; And break down its wall, and it shall be trampled down. I will lay it waste; It shall not be pruned or dug, But there shall come up briers and thorns. I will also command the clouds That they rain no rain on it." For the vineyard of the Lord of hosts is the house of Israel, And the men of Judah are His pleasant plant. He looked for justice, but behold, oppression; For righteousness, but behold, a cry for help." Isaiah 5:1-7 NKJV

This prophesy by Isaiah was for Israel and tells of a process not dis-similar to the description we see in Revelation, or for that matter some of Jesus' parables. Our focus will now turn sharply toward the area of the Church, but again you could use the same descriptions to better understand where Israel or Adam & Eve failed. Let us examine some of those parables or prophecies, because they will provide us the pattern or rhythm for Revelation. The story could basically sound as follows: that God owns or prepared a field or an area in the earth called the Church to influence all the Nations. He built into the field a wine press. In other words when the kingly grapes, or perfected Saints, representing Him mature they will be harvested and squeezed to produce kingly wine. It is what comes out of them when they are under pressure or experiencing bad circumstances that determine their kingly nature. In the middle of His field He places a watch tower and appoints overseers or managers over His Church. They must oversee the tilling of the field, planting, pruning, watering, fertilizing and harvesting of the kingly vine and grapes. But under the watchful eye of the overseers, the enemy manages to sneak in and plant non-kingly vines. The problem now, is if you try and pull out this vine of the enemy you might encumber or hurt the growth process of the kingly vine. To prevent this from happening God allows the side by side growth in the Church. When the kingly vine reaches maturity, when the number of the gentiles are full, He gives the instruction for the harvest to commence. Note however that in all instances the non-kingly grapes or fruits are always harvested and pressed first – producing un-palatable wine that has nothing royal that proceeds from within them. Only thereafter is the kingly harvest brought in to prepare what the Father set out to achieve in the first place. Note that during this entire process, there is nothing out of control or chaotic. It is a process that is happening in the full knowledge of the Father, that He allows to take place and it is completely under His control.

We are getting closer to one of the truths of the book of Revelation. And that is the question who is the book of Revelation intended for and what is the extent of its message? We might ask then also the question whether we should take the prophecies of the Book of Revelation and run to the World with it? Or is it something that we must take and run to other major religions with, such as to the Muslim communities? And the answer would be an emphatic - NO! This book of Revelation is as personal as God's intended instruction were to Adam & Eve, or God's law and first covenant was with Israel. You cannot see Israel running to their neighbour to their South, namely Egypt, with their received words from God – can you? Similarly the book of Revelation is written for a specific audience. And that audience is exclusively for the people in the Church, or for what we would term Christians. Therefore our focus must sharply turn to the ongoings, preparation and events that will happen and that is meant to effect the Church. Why you might ask is God's judgement commencing with His own people, or in His own field? Well quite simply it is for the same reason as to why God's judgement eventually turned to Adam & Eve or against Israel. They simply failed to fairly represent the heart and goodness of God the Father to their surrounding neighbours, tribes and nations. And inversely allowed their neighbours, other tribes and nations to inwardly influence them. Therefore, when it comes to the book of Revelation we have to sharply turn inward in the Church and ask if the pure woman represented in the sign of Revelation 12 has been replaced by the scarlet woman in Revelation 17. Let us look into this further. Because this is important to understand when we consider the prophecies.

God states in the book of 1 Peter that His judgement will always commence with His own people. And it has indeed been so since Jesus Christ ascended to heaven that a normal part of any Christian's growth path to perfection include as wilderness walk, or trials and tribulation or a crucible or a baptism of fire or any other way we want to describe this portion of the growth phase toward perfection. We then also see that the Apostles often penned down phrases such as "rejoice when you endure trials and tribulation because your perfection draws near". It then brings God's judgement into sharp focus if Revelation mentions that the trials and tribulations during these curtain drawing events, at the end of the age, will be the worst ever experienced by God's people:

"For the time has come for judgment to begin at the house of God; and if it begins with us first, what will be the end of those who do not obey the gospel of God?" I Peter 4:17 NKJV

But we might ask exactly what does this field comprise of or look like at this current moment. A report of the National Intelligence Council's 2020 Project – Mapping the Global Future – shows a Christian population in excess of 2,000 million people, expected to grow to in excess of 2,500 million in

2025 (NIC, 2004). I have included the populations from various religions from this report for your benefit in the accompanying graph. It is to these people, and their leadership especially, growing towards 2,500 million that the messages and events in Revelation is primarily pointed. What God is saying to us, is that for now He is OK with the rest of the world population and all the other religions. He is however growing weary with the Church and the people in it for not growing to truthfully represent Him in the Nations, as perfected saints, on the earth. And when we see Him speak out in Revelation it is God that effectively allows Satan himself to take-up a position of deceit in the Church for a period limited to three and a half years:

*"It was **granted to him** to make war with the saints and to overcome them. And authority was given him over every tribe, tongue, and nation. All who dwell on the earth will worship him, whose names have not been written in the Book of Life of the Lamb slain from the foundation of the world."* Revelation 13:7 - 8 NKJV

Number of Religious Adherents, 1900 - 2025

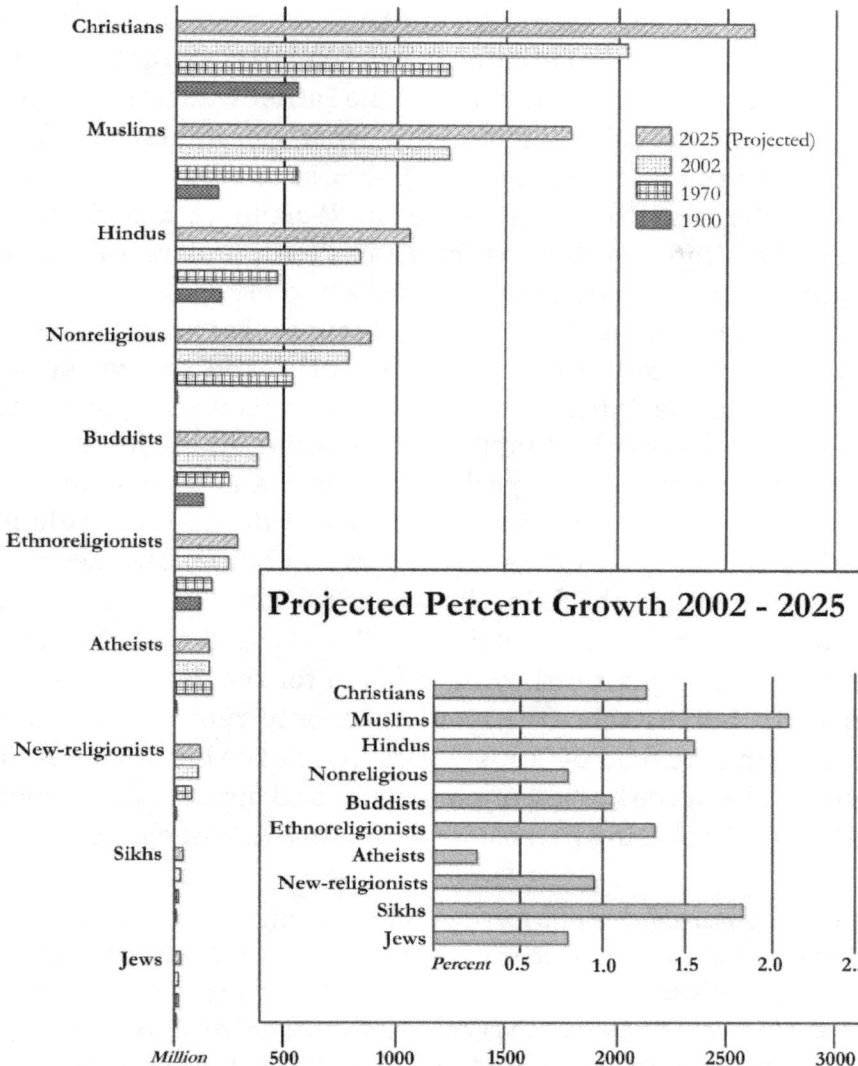

Legend:
- 2025 (Projected)
- 2002
- 1970
- 1900

Projected Percent Growth 2002 - 2025

Categories (inner chart):
Christians, Muslims, Hindus, Nonreligious, Buddists, Ethnoreligionists, Atheists, New-religionists, Sikhs, Jews

Percent axis: 0.5 1.0 1.5 2.0 2.5

Main chart categories: Christians, Muslims, Hindus, Nonreligious, Buddists, Ethnoreligionists, Atheists, New-religionists, Sikhs, Jews

Million axis: 500 1000 1500 2000 2500 3000

Source: Status and Trends Global Mission as Revealed by the Annual Christian Census, AD 1800-AD 2025, World Evangelization Research Centre

33

In comparison this is not unlike God allowing or sending Babylon in the Old Testament to invade Judah and Jerusalem and to kill them, annex them and carry them off to Babylon, all because of the shortfalls of their current and historic generations. We see therefore in parable after parable and in revelation after revelation that God the Father wants the Church to give Him, or cultivate for Him what He wants namely – perfected saints. If you are not 100% sure what this entails please refer also to *"Christian Unity: Walking in a motivating climate" by Hoffman Prinsloo* for an in depth understanding. If we for instance consider Jesus Christ's parable about the wheat and the tares you will be mistaken if you for instance conclude that the tares are the people in the world, and the wheat are the people in the Church. You will also be mistaken if you think the elected saints will be raptured first before all the impending trials and tribulations. A period three and a half years during which Satan or the deceiver is allowed to deceive and rule in the Church. Please meditate on the parable that follows. See that all these events in the field, the wheat and the tares, take place within the same field, namely the Church. And that the tares are removed only after they have fallen for the deceit of Satan, grown to harvestable fruit, and then only removed through either being crushed by Jesus Christ so that the blood comes up to the bridle of the horses, or plucked up and burnt as dead wood in the fire. A sobering parable if we read it with our eyes open:

"Another parable He put forth to them, saying: "The kingdom of heaven is like a man who sowed good seed in his field; but while men slept, his enemy came and sowed tares among the wheat and went his way. But when the grain had sprouted and produced a crop, then the tares also appeared. So the servants of the owner came and said to him, 'Sir, did you not sow good seed in your field? How then does it have tares?' He said to them, 'An enemy has done this.' The servants said to him, 'Do you want us then to go and gather them up?' But he said, 'No, lest while you gather

up the tares you also uproot the wheat with them. Let both grow together until the harvest, and at the time of harvest I will say to the reapers, "First gather together the tares and bind them in bundles to burn them, but gather the wheat into my barn." ' ""

Matthew 13:24-30 NKJV

If you are anything like me, with the mind of an engineer, you would want more details. We would want to ask ourselves, what percentage of the let's assume 2,500 million Christians qualifies as "wheat"? Again I believe Jesus gave us an insight into this question. In Matthew 24 Jesus goes into quite a bit of descriptive detail about the timing of the end time events, which we will consider a little later in greater detail. But he then suddenly switches in Matthew 25 when He tells the parable of the wise and foolish virgins. The first little word that He uses "Then" should make us sit upright and ask ourselves when is this "then"? And the answer, if you dissect what Jesus said in the foregoing chapter, is that this "then" of the parable is during the three and a half year tribulation period when Satan is allowed to rule and deceive in the Church. As we meditate then through this parable may our ears hear that these foretold events will be during the three and a half year tribulation period spoken of in the book of Revelation. And note that the coming of Christ is only at the end of this period. Note also, that there is no rapture before events preceding the second coming of Jesus Christ is concluded:

""Then the kingdom of heaven shall be likened to ten virgins who took their lamps and went out to meet the bridegroom. Now five of them were wise, and five were foolish. Those who were foolish took their lamps and took no oil with them, but the wise took oil in their vessels with their lamps. But while the bridegroom was delayed, they all slumbered and slept. "And at midnight a cry was heard: 'Behold, the bridegroom is coming; go out to meet him!' Then all those virgins arose and trimmed their lamps. And the foolish said to the wise, 'Give us some of your oil, for our lamps are going out.' But the wise answered, saying, 'No, lest there should not be enough for

us and you; but go rather to those who sell, and buy for yourselves.'
And while they went to buy, the bridegroom came, and those who
were ready went in with him to the wedding; and the door was shut.
"Afterward the other virgins came also, saying, 'Lord, Lord, open
to us!' But he answered and said, 'Assuredly, I say to you, I do not
know you.' "Watch therefore, for you know neither the day nor the
hour in which the Son of Man is coming." Matthew 25:1-13 NKJV

What now remains to be asked of the field, or the Church, is why approximately only 50% of the Christians are wise, and the other 50% are found to be foolish in the unfolding of these events. Perhaps also refer to "You are what you eat" by Hoffman Prinsloo in this search. But in short, at the end of times Christians are called to a similar time as in the times of Noah. And if we recall Noah, God sent warning of difficult times that was approaching because of God's ensuing judgement. And through repetitive warnings through Noah's father, grandfather and great grandfather Noah was to prepare a vessel of safety for his household. In those days it was to build a wooden boat to escape the perilous times. If Noah was not obedient, he and his family would have perished in the flood. It is very similar at the end of the age for each Church, the congregation, each family and each individual to build their figurative ark of safety. And that is done by growing perfected saints. If you do not achieve that prior to the coming of Satan and the three and a half year tribulation you will be delivered to be deceived if you are in the Church. There will be no more opportunity to prepare. Once you have repented and believe in your heart that Jesus is the Christ, then all the other faith steps of soul redemption through baptism in water and baptism in the Holy Spirt, heart redemption through morning by morning time building relationship with God the Father and redemption of the mind standing in trust or rest, quietness and confidence through difficult times is 100% in each believers hands through their leader or person they entrust to disciple them. And we simply have to take responsibility for our own lives and actions in these end of days. God is looking for perfected saints, meaning Saints that have grown through these processes, whose spiritual eyes and ears are opened and whom now as perfected Saints minister and serve in the body of Christ. A foolish virgin is one whose soul is not pointing to God the only good Father through baptism in water and in Spirit. And then having their vessels filled growing toward perfection. Please re-read this parable contemplatively as you think on the fact that these events occur during the tribulation, and only the wise saints consisting of approximately 50% meet their Saviour in His second coming.

We might now say that God is harsh. Or that the Church is still sleeping and very unaware of this. Or that the foolish 50% had very little warning, or bad leadership. But, let us remind ourselves that God our Father is a very merciful and compassionate Father. And in the run-up events to the deceit of Satan in the Church, the Saints will receive many opportunities to weigh the effectiveness of their doctrine to get their lives, families and congregations in order. The question however is: will they? We will discuss these eminent run-up events and the people in the Church's response thereto. But we can now already mark it in our memories that it is not God's lack of mercy or preparation time or lack of provision that will fall short, but rather the individual choices that remain 100% in the hands of each Saint every single day.

5 FOREST FOR
THE TREES

"**C**an't see the forest for the trees" mean that we are unable to understand a larger situation because we are focussing too much on the details in front of us. Therefore in order to understand this Church business better and accompanying events we have to zoom out completely and consider seven thousand years of Spiritual history by re-perusing from the beginning of Genesis to the end of Revelation. And what we find in the closing chapter of Revelation is descriptive words for a Tree of Life. And if we page to the opening Chapters of Genesis we encounter this same Tree of Life, or even better still this theme of trees in the garden of God or in the garden of Eden.

Now, I must admit that I am the first to confess that when I hear the story of Adam and Eve in the garden of Eden... I always but always imagined two people, Adam as a man and Eve as a woman, being the only two humans walking in a beautiful garden. And there were all kinds of fruit trees in the garden. I imagine green meandering grasslands and majestic waterfalls. And most often in this imaginary picture of mine there were no other people on the earth. Something picture perfect you would dream up at the start of a Walt Disney movie – don't you also imagine it so? My imaginary image would then go further that

Eve, when presented with a shiny red apple by the Serpent, sins by biting into the juicy apple. A type of fable that begins with once upon a time...

Well let me shock you as I was shocked when I started getting the Revelation of this. Just one of the problems with this image is that suddenly when Adam and Eve left their paradise there were seemingly all kinds of other people on the Earth. Just think on that for a moment... Adam and Eve's sons managed to find wives outside Eden that somehow must have appeared mysteriously! Allow me to start telling a different tale. Once you are shocked, as I was, we can expand the theme of the story to encompass a wider period, including some Bible texts... and then hopefully a clear picture will start forming in our minds.

A long, long, time ago... there was a man and a woman called Adam and Eve. You could say they were like a kind of king over a land with similar boundaries which much later years a certain guy with the name Moses claimed God Himself gave to a nation called Israel. The land's boundaries were the same Canaan boundaries that God the Father promised to a person named Abraham some centuries earlier. The woman Eve was tasked by her Father God to fairly represent His sanctuary in heaven that He gave her a glimpse of. A tree was planted on this land, which roots spread through all the corners of this piece of land. The tree grew and was called the Tree of Life. And the fruits and leaves from this tree was to be given to citizens of the adjacent Nations in that area. This entire area that encompassed numerous Nations, including the land that the Tree of Life was planted on, was called Eden or "the garden of God". However there was as in any good story a problem. In close proximity to the tree of life in Eden, another Nation or tree was planted. This Nation was called Tyre. This Nation's king used to be perfect, so much so that he was even claimed to have the status of a select few of the most intimate and powerful angels of God. Most of the trade in those days went through this Nation. And soon the king of Tyre grew in pride and started focussing more on the riches of this Nation, which included all kinds of lucrative relationships, finances and physical health than on his relationship with God. This tree grew. It was also given a sanctuary that was initially a carbon copy of the example shown them in heaven. Well it was not long before Woman from the Tree of Life area came over to this Tyre Nation and was presented with and her eyes opened to the fruit of tree of Good and Evil. Even though she was pure and had clear instructions not to bite into the fruit of this greedy and prideful Nation – she was overcome by her temptation. Rather than offering the citizens of that Nation the fruit from the tree of Good and Evil as per her mandate she chose to eat their fruit. There were at that time many other Nations or trees planted in that region of Eden other than the Tree of Life and the Tree of Good and Evil. After ruining her own day by biting into the fruits from this Nation Tyre, she offered some also to her husband back in the land she originated from. Unfortunately because of this both the king and herself as the representative sanctuary for the Tree of Life was thrown out of their land and prevented from returning. That was done because everyone was afraid that if they eat of the fruit from this Tree of Life... they would live forever in their corrupted state.

This story of the trees sounds like fiction or like a fable, right? If we move forward in time we later see that Abraham, Izak and Jacob (renamed Israel) became and was planted in that same land Israel as the roots to a tree. Much later as the tree grew and after the failure of Israel, the trunk of the tree became represented by a man called Jesus Christ as descendant of king David of Israel. A tree with twelve of its natural branches growing out into all the wind directions. It started growing taller and taller and its branches started reaching other Nations. Note however the tree trunk was near terminated when two new woman, one for the nation Israel and one for the nation Judah, representing the sanctuary areas respectively established in Samaria and in Jerusalem went prostituting with its neighbouring Nations. These two woman as Eve did went eating the fruits from neighbouring trees ... rather than offering fruit from their own Tree of Life. Following this event the twelve branches from the Tree of Life was pruned and set aside. For a third time the gardener re-established the trunk of the Tree of Life. This time however with the Gardener working through a sanctuary called the Church to engraft foreign twigs onto the tree. With continuous watering this tree has grown to reach Nations in the furthest corners of the Globe.

We should note that God Himself is the owner of the land or claimed it as His inheritance. Even though portions of the land owned by God is illegitimately occupied by people, no other Nation or tree will ever be allowed to root on this land. Reason being that land annexed illegally is required for the roots of the Tree of Life in order to grow its branches, sprout leaves and fruits to reach all other Nations for healing and for fruit to eat. The woman or sanctuary, is a tool in the hand of the Gardener, and responsible for the in-grafting of new individual twigs from Nations onto the Tree of Life. The mandate of the woman is to in-graft individuals from Nations and oversee their growth until they yield fruit and leaves themselves. They can however only grow and bloom if they receive sustenance from the living waters that mysteriously run only under the Promised land. This living water is taken up through the roots of the tree, and through the tree-trunk providing life-giving sustenance to the in-grafted branches.

If the woman allocated this role solicit with the Nations and grow fruit with them, she is acting more like a prostitute. Growing and eating from the fruits of the Nations. But imagine a pure Sister engrafting twigs from the Nations onto the branches of the Tree of Life that reached those Nations. A sister that oversees the in-grafting of each individual twig and nurturing until each matures and yields its fruit and leaves for the healing of that Nation. Fruit that gives of an aroma and taste – fit for a King!

The relevance of all of this "tree stuff" to our study, before we continue our further perusal of Revelation, include ideas that we have to consider. The physical land and boundaries of the land of Israel as promised to Abraham, and with borders originally given to Moses in the Old Testament is extremely important. It is important because that land belongs to only one person, and that is God the Father. We should be certain that that is not someone that any man, tribe, language or Nation would want to mess with – release His land to Him, for He has good intention with it for all the Nations. He planted a tree on this land, and no matter what we do as humans, or tribes or Nations that Tree of Life will root there, and grow from there into a mighty tree. The twelve tribes of Israel will be grafted into that tree. And as the tree grows and reaches all the Nations, individual citizens from those Nations will be in-grafted on that tree to not only bear fruit but also bear leaves. The ingested fruit will turn more citizens from those Nations to be in-grafted and the accompanying leaves will be for the healing of those Nations. The tree is purposed by God the Father to extend shade, safety, healing and fruits for the Nations' benefit.

With that picture in mind of this Tree of Life being beneficial to all the Nations, one is dumb-struck to think why any Nation, tribe or people would not want to see to it that the land is cleared only for God's purposes, or why the branches would be persecuted, or the fruit and the leaves shunned. It must be something more sinister in motivation if the only motive of the Tree of Life is to bring only good to the Nations – don't you think? It smacks of something like self-mutilation or masochism if any Nation works against the effective rooting and growth of this tree.

The prostitute woman currently representing the sanctuary which should be responsible for individuals in Nations to be in-grafted and matured until they, not the woman, bear fruit and leaves is an entire different matter. If she is found to be mis-representing God the Father's intentions God's judgement, fury and vengeance will be unleashed on this prostitute woman. God will do that by sending a powerful deception into her, to deceive all members that choose to remain in her. The Nations itself with whom she is soliciting, idolising and forming a unity is destined to turn on her and to destroy her. That in essence is the main theme of Revelation.

6 THEBEAST FROM THE SEA

"For God has put it into their hearts to fulfil His purpose... until the words of God are fulfilled" Revelation 17: 17

Probably one of the key descriptions to try and fathom in the book of Revelation is the image of the Beast that rises from the sea as described in Revelation 13: 1 to 10. This is the same red dragon described in Revelation 12: 3 and 4 and later coloured in in Revelation 17 when described as the scarlet beast. The identifying traits, in all these above referenced verses, are that this beast, or red dragon or scarlet beast has the following qualities including:

1. Seven heads: are seven mountains;
2. Seven heads: are also seven kings and when John was shown the Revelation five have fallen, one was and the seventh one had yet to come;
3. The body of the Beast itself: is himself also the eight;
4. Ten horns: are ten kings that has not received a kingdom yet in the days of John receiving the Revelation, but receive authority for one hour with the Beast.

If as Christians we wish to understand the sequence of Revelation and the times that we are living in, this image of the Beast from the Sea and subsequently the city Babylon that comes forth from the "harlotry" between the scarlet woman sitting on this scarlet beast that is described in Revelation 17 is one of the keys to try and understand. One could build a case and believe that this image is purely a spiritual image, and that one would not find anything physical to trace this appearance of the Beast by. But that is possibly not entirely true, and one can sense looking at history and current evidence that it is a mixture of the spiritual and visible fleshly truths.

Often times when dealing with Biblical prophecy, especially when relating to the prophecies at the end of the ages, one has to ask the crucial question: where is the United States of America in Biblical prophecy? And many writers, especially those based in the USA do pose that question and proceed to answer that. Often times the "young lions" in Old Testament Scripture is used to refer to the United States, when they complain when Israel is attacked. But one senses that the young lions could rather be the Suni Muslims whom recently warmed again in their trade relationships with Israel. Or in other instances Tarshish and the ships of Tarshish is referred to as the role of the USA. But one has to wonder where is the USA as "friend of Israel" or this super power as we have come to know it in modern times when Biblical end times prophecies are considered? It simply does not make sense if you do not bring the USA into the mix in your consideration of the Global impact of events foreseen.

If you start musing and consider all the modern geo-political, economic and current affairs in the World, and start using wisdom to build a picture and relate this back to Biblical prophecy a sobering picture starts to immerse. Try and use your imagination as the following descriptive scenario is painted below. Imagine that the seven heads of the Beast becoming visible in front of your view is the seven continents as we now know them. Mountains or high places in revelation normally indicate sanctuaries from where offering and sacrifices are made to their gods. With these seven heads also represented in part by the early Biblical prophecies of Daniel where we can muse that these heads of the Beast are represented by the following kingdoms as they emerge and dissipate:

1. Kingdom 1: Babylon - gold;
2. Kingdom 2: Medo-Persia - silver;
3. Kingdom 3: Greece – bronze;
4. Kingdom 4: Roman - iron;
5. Kingdom 5: Roman Empire – iron mixed with clay
6.   Kingdom 6: Medieval Age commences in 476 after Christ with the fall of the Roman Empire;
7.   Kingdom 7: Modern Age where Europe colonialize countries and America is discovered in 1492 after Christ;

In your imagination of this Beast, think that each of these kingdoms, or seven heads, defined unique attributes towards how a modern human superpower's values are entrenched. You could reason that the kingdom of Babylon contributed toward the understanding of a global economy. You could reason that the kingdom of Mede-Persia contributed toward the understanding of a war machine. How the kingdom of Greece contributed towards the culture of writing, philosophy, maths and arts and culture. Or how the Roman, and Roman Empire contributed toward the way financial accounting is done globally or perhaps the interplay between state and church is understood or the legal system operates. And so on.

This beast is a human effort and way of building a world dominating kingdom, consisting of culture, politics, financial systems, a war machine and economy. Then perhaps in the 1940's after Pearl Harbour is bombed, the Japanese Empire in the Hollywood movie Midway correctly speaks the words "today we have awoken the Beast". We could imagine that the body of this Beast is the United States of America our modern superpower born out of and improving the best that previous powers developed. Our first response would certainly be – it cannot be! Surely the USA represent liberty, is the most democratic empire ever, is a representation of Christianity worldwide etc. Its modern military prowess surely represents the image of a righteous, clean, big brother for all the oppressed in the World one might argue?

But, meditate on it for a bit whilst you hold this image of the Beast in your mind, with its seven heads and the United States of America as its body – the Beast itself. We are not talking here of a specific people, or saying that Americans or for that matter Christian Americans are evil. What we are contemplating is two opposing Kingdoms. One being the Kingdom of God, and how mature Christians or ambassadors of this Kingdom build culture, finance, economics, relationships, laws etc. Compared to a worldly kingdom that was built on the principles of seven preceding kingdoms and now culminated in the Beast itself as the climax human-kingdom, not to be surpassed by anything else we can muster up in our human efforts. That is the Beast... it is the human way of building the ultimate kingdom with the fingerprints of humans all over it, and the spirit of Satan breathed into the image of the Beast. If you as I did struggle with this realisation, perhaps go back to the image of the Tree of Life. This tree is rooted in the Isreal land, not in the USA. This tree's branches grow and reach the USA. Christians in the USA are ingrafted by the pure woman and grown to maturity on the branches of the Tree of Life to yield fruit and leaves for the healing of the USA. But the USA itself can and never will be the where the Tree of Life is rooted, and ultimately is only a human superpower Nation.

The final chapter of the growth of this Beast is with the unity found between ten horns or Nations that grows from or on the body of the Beast. Importantly we should note that these ten scales form part of the Beast which if we muse on it wisely cannot be divided against itself. In the book of Revelation these ten horns are given to us as a "timing" occurrence, by which we can measure ensuing events. The first of these horns on the Beast commences and is already prophesied in the old Testament in Ezekiel 38 and essentially make the core of the unity of the ten horns, when they attack Israel in the end days (we can suspect at the end of the reign of the anti-Christ) including:

1. Horn 1: Russia;
2. Horn 2: Turkey;
3. Horn 3: Iran;
4. Horn 4: Ethiopia;
5. Horn 5: Libia;

And we can surely muse further, contemplate and instinctively feel and imagine that the formation of the BRICS grouping is now completing the picture of these ten horns forming unity at the end of days, including:

6. Horn 6: Brazil;
7. Horn 7: India;
8. Horn 8: China;
9. Horn 9: South Africa;
10. Horn 10: We can muse Egypt or other.

If you ponder it there will be common threads that will cause the final kingdoms to form unity. It could be that they will find communism or autocratic rule not too an uncomfortable ideology. That they rely on natural resources to drive their principle economy as opposed to green energy. That inherently they will ultimately hate the church or rather the prostitute sister of the church. Because they will turn on and fulfil God's purposes to destroy this non-representative sanctuary.

The qualities of these last ten kingdoms that will ultimately give their authority to the body of the Beast, in our imaginary picture the USA, is described to have the following characteristics including:

- They will in the end hate the harlot (the Scarlet woman or the religious based Church if you will), make her desolate, and naked, eat her flesh and burn her with fire. And although this harlot Woman was greatly responsible in creating the might of the beast, and although these

Countries thrive off of this system created by the Beast, these ten kingdoms are still destined by God Himself to punish this harlot Woman. If you contemplate each of these Countries on the list of ten, one can only muse why each individual Country ultimately hates the false (religious) Church or scarlet woman. It could be that the Country is Muslim, or radical Muslim, or the Country is Communist or the Country ultimately sees the Church as the ultimate force behind Colonialism... but in their unity, there is a profound and deep down hatred and resentment toward the scarlet Woman.

- These ten kingdoms are of one mind. And one can imagine that in terms of economy, financial systems, culture, and political will they will form a unity and one front to influence Global decision making.
- They ultimately, beyond all the smoke screens, play into the hand of the Beast and give the authority of their kingdoms to the Beast. Ultimately the seven heads, the body of the beast and the ten horns jointly form the Beast, or counterfeit kingdom, in contrast to the Kingdom of God.

The purpose of this knowledge is not to single out the USA or South Africa or China or Russia or a colonialising Europe... but rather to see that human history, culture, self-determination, ambition, survival instincts, power struggles, or call out whatever human trait you will, has created this Beast seen in Revelation rising out of the waters (signifying all seven continents and every tongue, tribe and nation). The lateness of the hour that we are living in signify that the body of the Beast is the United States of America which all can already see is heading towards decline. More importantly in terms of Revelation timing the final ten horns, or Nations, utilising and launching off of the values and systems created by the USA should be sobering to all of us. If there is only one message that you take out of this Chapter, it should be - the hour is late. Sketching this Beast for ourselves will help us tremendously in our reading

49

and contemplation of Revelation if we encounter this Beast in Revelation 12, 13 and 17 with its seven heads, its body and ten horns, represented as follows:

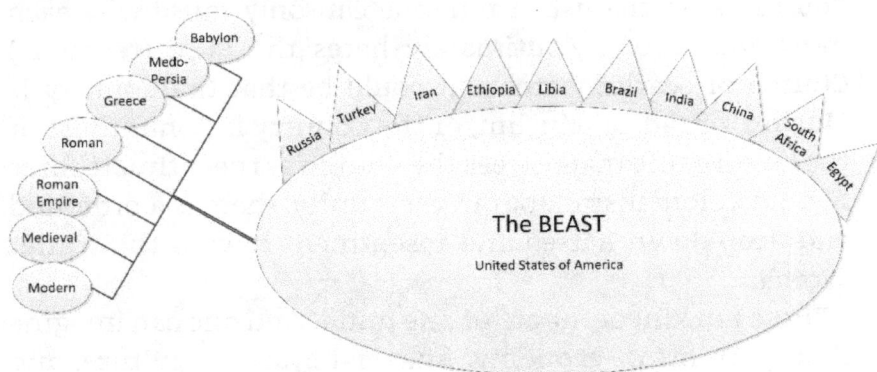

From our earlier contemplation, we considered that the Woman (in this case the harlot) sits on top of the Beast (in this case the definitive human kingdom with its body represented by the United States of America). The children from their fornication ultimately produces fruit or actions which produce a City – Babylon. In other words with the Woman (a human religious Church not representing the Spiritual Church) choosing to align with this human inspired kingdom and their subsequent fornication produces children building the ultimate human city – most probably a New York. Contemplate this, that this ultimate representation of culture, money, economics, political systems eventually manifests in a tangible city – namely New York City. It sounds absolutely ludicrous if we read it here – but as we meditate on it and realize that the New York stock exchange, banking systems, with the International Monetary Fund, the World Bank, the United Nations headquarters, etc. are all domiciled in New York... our initial denial response starts to slowly dwindle. And we start realising that all our human efforts to build our own kingdom with all our own religious interpretations and understanding, ultimately culminates into something that looks, feels, sounds, tastes and is pretty much representative of a New York. It does not get any higher or more real than this as far as our own human efforts are concerned. That city is compared to the true spiritual church or pure Woman, sitting on the Kingdom of God, producing children whose actions and works assist to form a New Jerusalem described at the end of the book of Revelation.

We might not have all the names of the heads or horns on the Beast out of the Sea correct... and you can play around with your own version of it. The important concept to grasp here is that each head of the Beast contributed a specific quality leading to the ultimate body of the Beast. What we should grasp is that this Beast is representative of the worldly kingdom systematically built up over the rise and fall of numerous world dominating cultures. The most important and final contemplation of this Chapter is the following: if we can already see the body of the Beast, and more vitally already see the formation of the unity of its final ten horns or kingdoms and already see the city Babylon... how close are we to the final events that play out in the book of Revelation?

7 THE SALT

One of the better descriptions I have seen depicting the unfolding events of the Revelation prophecy was that of a Pastor using a salt dispenser and a pepper dispenser. We will therefore focus on the Salt, Pepper and the combined Salt & Pepper analogy in the next few chapters. They are immensely important in the understanding of Revelation.

The Salt for our purposes is represented by the three persons of the Trinity, namely God the Father, Jesus Christ and the Holy Spirit. And the salt dispenser represent the second coming of Jesus Christ. Although John is not as descriptive in Revelation of the Father, Jesus Christ and the Holy Spirit as he is in describing Satan as the Dragon, the first Beast from the sea and the second Beast from the earth, it is still very important to describe God, Jesus and the Holy Spirit in the Revelation context for ourselves. I suspect John did not do that in such great detail because he assumes the reader of Revelation is already familiar with these three Persons of which we form a description for ourselves.

God the Father

If we have to contemplate some characteristics of God the Father for the end of the age there are so many things we can say about God the Father. But as the times accelerate and we start experiencing a rushing as if a river is in full flood and passing by rapidly, we should perhaps focus on the following characteristics including:

1. God's mercy and compassion towards His people during the end of the ages increase exponentially;
2. Even if times and events accelerate God will never pressure us to choose Him, but always allow us to willingly choose Him and grow by the choosing of our own will;
3. God remains 100% in control, in-fact He eventually, when events culminates, is the one that allows for the deception to take place in the area of the Church.

Bind these three thoughts in your mind, we will step over them again. But this sets the modus operandi of God the Father apart from any other during the end times events. The enemy cannot imitate these aspects of God the Father. As events unfold God will use His matured or "perfected" saints to show and lead younger Christians to maturity and safety, thereby showing His mercy and compassion. He will, unlike His enemy, never rush you to take a decision for Him or to grow in Him. He will not push you, or force you, or extort you, or threaten you at any time, but always allow you to wilfully choose Him. We could say that when there are much louder voices, He always whispers.

If I had to choose one string of Bible texts to best describe God's character it would be 1 Corinthians 13: 4 to 7. You can definitely read the verse, as intended, on how we should try and attain to become love. But at the same time, it is also meant to reflect who we are to become like – namely like God our Father. Therefore read with me 1 Corinthians 13: 4 to 7 to get a true reflection of what God the Father is like:

"Love suffers long and is kind; love does not envy; love does not parade itself, is not puffed up; does not behave rudely, does not seek its own, is not provoked, thinks no evil; does not rejoice in iniquity, but rejoices in the truth; bears all things, believes all things, hopes all things, endures all things."

I Corinthians 13:4-7 NKJV

This image you get of God the Father in the description of love we just read is supported by the texts describing God visiting Abraham. The Bible in Genesis 12: 7 (KJV) states:

> *"And the Lord appeared unto Abraham, and said: 'Unto thy seed will I give this land' and there builded he an altar unto the Lord, who appeared unto him."* Now burn the following image of God into your meditation:
> *"and he sat in the tent door in the heat of the day (in the desert); and he lift up his eyes and looked, and, lo, three men stood by him: and when he saw them, he ran to meet them from the tent door, and bowed himself toward the ground... let a little water, I pray you, be fetched, and wash your feet, and rest under the tree: and I will fetch a morsel of bread – so that you can regain your power. And he took butter, milk and the calf which he had dressed, and set it before them; and he stood by them under the tree, and they did eat".*

Now, this image of God does not fit the image of lightening, power and top of the ladder stuff, does it? No, this image of God, in fact, fits the image of Jesus washing His disciples' dirty feet in John 13: 1 to 17 (KJV):

> *"...your Lord and Master, have washed your feet; ye also ought to wash one another's feet... the servant is not greater than his lord; neither he that is sent greater than he that sent him."*

In the Genesis text we witness God as He sits on the ground – his feet and face dirty and sweaty; he eats bread, milk, and meat under a tree...hot, hungry, and humble. Wow. Not the image the world at large portrays of God, is it?

God appears in a gentle whisper: 1 Kings 19: 12 to 13:

> *"After the earthquake came a fire, but the Lord was not in the fire. And after the fire came a gentle whisper. When Elijah heard it, he pulled his cloak over his face and went out and stood at the mouth of the cave. Then a voice said to him, 'What are you doing here, Elijah?"'*

Because the book of Revelation revolves around deception that is to come, it is imperative that we draw an exceedingly clear and concise image of God. For this purpose, and pardon me for being presumptuous, we will name God and give Him an image so that we may envision the time, events and strategies with uniformed clarity. For this purpose and in the Spirit of Truth, we choose the following name and image:

Name: Yahweh or meaning, I was what I was, I am what I am, and will be what I will be, forever. How about that for a code name?

Works Associated to God: From a definition standpoint, it is very important that you internalise exactly what the key functions of God are in the process or order of the Christian. As part of the Holy Trinity, God is responsible for **Mercy and Love** – it has much to do with your **heart**. Remember this vital concept.

Image: Let us choose the code image for God – represented by the picture below, so that there can be no misunderstanding later.

GOD (the Father)

The most important aspect about God the Father that we need to understand through experience is that He is relational. We get to know Him when we spend day-by-day unhurried time with Him in the secret place praising, worshipping, praying, reading the Word, meditating and simply spending our most precious daily quality time with Him.

Jesus Christ

David wrote that we must praise God in His sanctuary, praise God in the constellation and praise God for His works of faithfulness here on the earth. I once did an exercise where as I read the Bible from beginning to the end, it was with the intention of drawing up an Excel spreadsheet timeline for myself. In the most left column I named the person, example Adam, or Noah or Abraham or the kings of Judah, or the prophets. And then mark each person's time out on a time roster commencing from the year zero up to the current day say for example 2025 or the Jewish year 5785. The whole focus of my meditation was to plot the fulfilment of the promise of Christ, which happened in our modern year zero or more or less in the Jewish calendar year 3760. If you want to really see the mercy, the goodness and the faithfulness of God in order to sing His praise here on the earth, looking back 2000 years to the birth of Christ and then looking even further back to the events, promises and prophecies for another 3760 years, all the way back to Adam, it is simply indescribable in words alone. You have to break out in praise. And this Christ's name was Jesus the son of God our Father.

God is glorified through the Spirit. Jesus Christ Himself called it the Law of the Spirit. Romans 8: 2 (NIV) states that:

"through Christ Jesus the law of the Spirit who gives life
has set you free from the law of sin and death."

After the fall of man, our nature changed; we were no longer of the Spirit but of the world – our carnal nature leading to sin and death. Behind each law, the Spiritual nature as opposed to our carnal nature, sits a god which is glorified. Behind the Spiritual nature is God and behind our carnal nature is Satan. Because of this shift in our essence, we (fallen man) naturally crave the visible, audible, tangible and material. Unfortunately for us these two natures cannot co-exist, because our obsession for the material (or Satan behind it) brings enmity between us and God (who is Spiritual in nature).

As we continue the description of the Revelation characters it becomes imperative that we clearly define each character and link the name, image and work associated with each into one representation. This is important in order to avoid any confusion that will set in as the Revelation plot unfolds. The name and image we choose associated with Jesus follows:

Name: Jesus Christ

Works associated to Jesus Christ: From a definition standpoint, it is very important that you know exactly what the key functions of Jesus are in the process or order of the Christian. As part of the Holy Trinity, Jesus is responsible for **Faith and Grace** – which has much to do with your **mind**. Remember this vital concept.

Image: Let us choose a code image for Jesus – represented by the picture below, so that there can be no misunderstanding later.

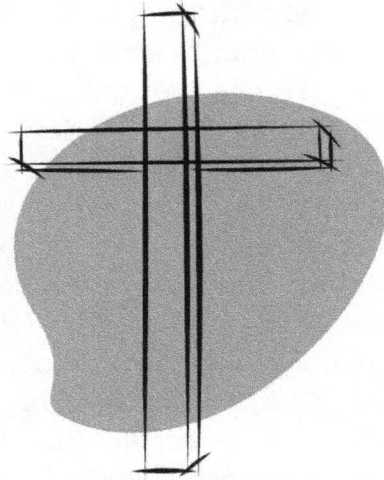

JESUS (the Son)

Jesus also set up the altar, obviously at the foot of the cross, and brought the final and ultimate sin offering outside the camp for you and me – Himself.

Jesus brought us two seminal things (refer John 1: 14 and 17) that we could not access prior to His birth, life, crucifixion, death, burial, resurrection and ascension:

1. **The Truth**: Jesus unlocked a gate for us into the Holy of Holies. The Holy Spirit is a wind; it blows us where we cannot go on our own. Now, we have a pathway to God, albeit it one that can be arduous at times. From the parable of the prodigal son, as told by Jesus, we intuitively feel that our return journey starts far from home, but that we now have access to the Father:

    "But while he was still a long way off, his father saw him and was filled with compassion for him; he [the father] ran to his son [you and me], threw his arms around him and kissed him [relieved that you are now safe]" Luke 15: 20 (NIV).

    Also refer to John 14: 16 and 17 and John 16: 13 which clearly show that Jesus brought us Truth by sending us the Spirit:

"And I will ask the Father, and he will give you another
advocate to help you and be with you forever – the
Spirit of truth. The world cannot accept him, because
it neither sees him nor knows him. But you know him,
for he lives with you and will be in you" and
"But when he, the Spirit of truth, comes, he will guide you
into all the truth. He will not speak on his own; he will speak
only what he hears, and he will tell you what is yet to come."

2. **The Grace**: Jesus positions a cross or a visible sign for all human beings to observe. For some it is a cross, for some a date, yet for others it is the reference to Christ in history AD and BC. But, somewhere in your life, you will see the reference to Christ even if you choose to ignore it. Think of it as a cross on the distant horizon, a beacon calling you to the edge.

3.

"The Lord said to Moses, 'Make a snake and put it up on
a pole; anyone who is bitten can look at it and live'"
Numbers 21: 8 (NIV).

For our study of the book of Revelation Jesus Christ's own words in Matthew 24 and 25 is of cardinal importance. Firstly because there Jesus Himself gives us a timing of events. But more importantly tells us of His second coming – what it will be like. Unlike anything else that anybody in the form of a movie, a book, a sermon or any other form of communication of advertisement would want to show you Jesus Christ is very clear on what His coming will be like. Read His own description here, and burn this into your memory, because it is unlike any other way that a deceiver will want to make you believe:

*""**Immediately after the tribulation** of those days the sun*
will be darkened, and the moon will not give its light; the
stars will fall from heaven, and the powers of the heavens

59

> *will be shaken. Then the **sign of the Son of Man will appear in heaven**, and then **all the tribes of the earth will mourn**, and **they will see the Son of Man coming on the clouds of heaven with power and great glory**. And He **will send His angels with a great sound of a trumpet**, and they will **gather together His elect from the four winds**, from one end of heaven to the other."* Matthew 24:29-31 NKJV

These verses from Jesus describing His own second coming is so clear and so descriptive in terms of the timing, or the when, the signs in heaven and the global scale of the event accompanied by sounds and sights that it will be un-mistakeable. Should we be part of the rapture theorists, saying that the Christian will be raptured before the tribulation, Jesus' words here spoils it for us, doesn't it?

The Holy Spirit

Unfortunately for us the Holy Spirit is introduced to us very late in Scripture when Jesus Christ promises Him to us as a gift after Jesus' accension. However the Spirit is mentioned numerous times in the Old Testament, but not in great enough detail for us to form an exact picture of Him, we might argue?. But, every time Israel or Judah is depicted as a woman we must know that the Spirit was inferred. Remember our earlier Revelation analogy that the pure Woman rides on a Kingdom and has off-spring that then ultimately form a city - Jerusalem? That picture should come to mind every time God refers to Israel or Judah as a woman in the Old Testament. We should note however our Old Testament argument regarding the Holy Spirit is not complete unless we realise that the entire Proverbs 8 deals exclusively with the Holy Spirit, who He is, what He is like, His love towards us, and His character – please spend some time with this Scripture in Proverbs until it becomes your own.

The Holy Spirit of God if depicted similarly in the context of a Beast, that the pure woman rides on, consists of the seven heads and the body of the Beast. The Holy Spirit being the seven heads (or rather a better analogy is the seven lamps from the lampstand in the Tabernacle) and the eight, the body of the Beast, is the Spirit of God Himself or the Kingdom of God. These seven Spirits are described by Isaiah as follows:

1. The Spirit of the Lord that rests on me.
2. The Spirit of knowledge that fills me (my soul).
3. The Spirit of wisdom that fills me (my heart).
4. The Spirit of understanding that fills me (my mind).
5. The Spirit of council that fills me.
6. The Spirit of might that fills me.
7. And the Spirit of the fear of God that fills me.

Because Revelation is a book on war and strategy, it is important for us to have a very clear and concise image of the Holy Spirit. For this purpose and in the Spirit of Truth, we choose the following name and image:

Name: Holy Spirit of Yahweh or meaning, the Holy Spirit of I was what I was, I am what I am, and will be what I will be, forever.

Works Associated to Holy Spirit: From a definition point, it is very crucial that you know exactly what the key functions of the Holy Spirit are in the process or order of the Christian. As part of the Holy Trinity, the Holy Spirit is responsible for **Power** and **Truth, Goodness, Knowledge, Obedience, Perseverance** that through trials leads to **Hope** – it has much to do with the knowledge of the **salvation of your soul**. Remember this fundamentally-important concept.

Image: Let us choose a code image for the Holy Spirit, represented by the picture below, so that there can be no misunderstanding later.

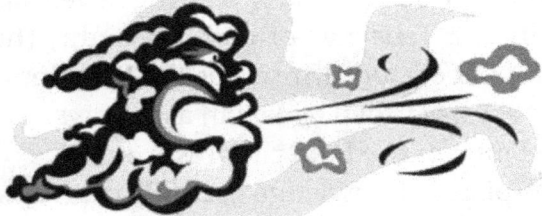

The HOLY SPIRIT

Perhaps at this stage take a break and read either Proverbs 8 or Romans 8: 1 to 17 (NIV) below, to refresh your thoughts and to meditate on the true intentions of the Holy Spirit:

"Therefore, there is now no condemnation for those who are in Christ Jesus, because through Christ Jesus the law of the Spirit who gives life has set you free from the law of sin and death. For what the law was powerless to do because it was weakened by the flesh, God did by sending his own Son in the likeness of sinful flesh to be a sin offering. And so he condemned sin in the flesh, in order that the righteous requirement of the law might be fully met in us, who do not live according to the flesh but according to the Spirit. Those who live according to the flesh have their minds set on what the flesh desires; but those who live in accordance with the Spirit have their minds set on what the Spirit desires. The mind governed by the flesh is death, but the mind governed by the Spirit is life and peace. The mind governed by the flesh is hostile to God; it does not submit to God's law, nor can it do so. Those who are in the realm of the flesh cannot please God. You, however, are not in the realm of the flesh but are in the realm of the Spirit, if indeed the Spirit of God lives in you. And if anyone does not have the Spirit of Christ, they do not belong to Christ. But if Christ is in you, then even though your body is subject to death because of sin, the Spirit gives life because of righteousness. And if the Spirit of him who raised Jesus from the dead is living in you, he who raised Christ from the dead will also give life to your mortal bodies because of his Spirit who lives in you. Therefore, brothers and sisters, we have an obligation

– but it is not to the flesh, to live according to it. For if you live according to the flesh, you will die; but if by the Spirit you put to death the misdeeds of the body, you will live. For those who are led by the Spirit of God are the children of God. The Spirit you received does not make you slaves, so that you live in fear again; rather, the Spirit you received brought about your adoption to sonship. And by him we cry, 'Abba, Father.' The Spirit himself testifies with our spirit that we are God's children. Now if we are children, then we are heirs – heirs of God and co-heirs with Christ, if indeed we share in his sufferings in order that we may also share in his glory."

What we have done so far in this chapter is to assign a name, a description and a picture that describes God the Father, Jesus Christ and the Holy Spirit. John did not sketch these pictures in Revelation. We are doing it here in order to make it easier for us to distinguish the flow of events described in the Revelation scriptures. One thing that is important for us to grasp here is the question of a mark on the forehead or a mark on the right hand. If you are redeemed in your soul, by the Holy Spirit, redeemed in your heart by God the Father, and redeemed in your mind by Jesus Christ you are in Revelation speak marked on your forehead and on your right hand. The number 7-7-7 depicts as per our illustration below the following:

First 7: is the "beast" or Kingdom of God the Father. The Kingdom is the body of the beast where God the Father is seated on His mercy throne. The Kingdom is lead by seven heads representing the Holy Spirit including the Spirit of the Lord, the Sprit of knowledge, the Spirit of wisdom, the Spirit of understanding, the Spirit of council, the Spirit of might or strength and the Spirit of the fear of God. Note carefully that this is a Spiritual Kingdom, given direction by the Holy Spirit.

Second 7: is the pure or Spiritual Church represented by the pure woman that sits on the beast or Kingdom of God. In Bible language the pure woman "knows" the Kingdom or has intimate communion with the Kingdom and becomes impregnated. The children that the woman brings forth is perfected saints or mature Christians (that has been discipled through the Spiritual growth phases of infant, young man, father and perfected saint).

Third 7: is the works of these saints that build a road, that later becomes a highway... or as Isaiah would put it eventually becomes a highway of holiness. Also their actions and works build and cover the city that is being built, each with a small pure, white, line cloth. We can call the city by names including the great city, the holy Jerusalem or the New Jerusalem. The name Zion is reserved for the high place or the sanctuary. Ultimately this new city depicts the woman that is given to Christ Jesus as His reward whom He marries as per Revelation 21: 9 and 10.

The mark 7 – 7 – 7 therefore consists of being a citizen of the Kingdom of Heaven, born from the pure Woman (the child matured in soul, heart, mind and serving diligently in the Christian community), and can enter the city New Jerusalem. Any mature Christian that has gone through such a Spiritual growth process to maturity, as more broadly described in *"You are what you eat"* by Hoffman Prinsloo or *"Christian Unity: Walking in a motivating climate"* by Hoffman Prinsloo, is marked by this number. Note however, you can walk up to any such a Christian today and realise that you cannot see these numbers on their forehead or even on their right hand. These are markings visible only in the spiritual world. However, these marking are there to "see" with Spiritual eyes.

Now if we contemplate and we know that the end days will be filled with deceit, or efforts to imitate God's intention with a false version or replica, then the following depiction of the Kingdom of God that the we should know is depicted as follows:

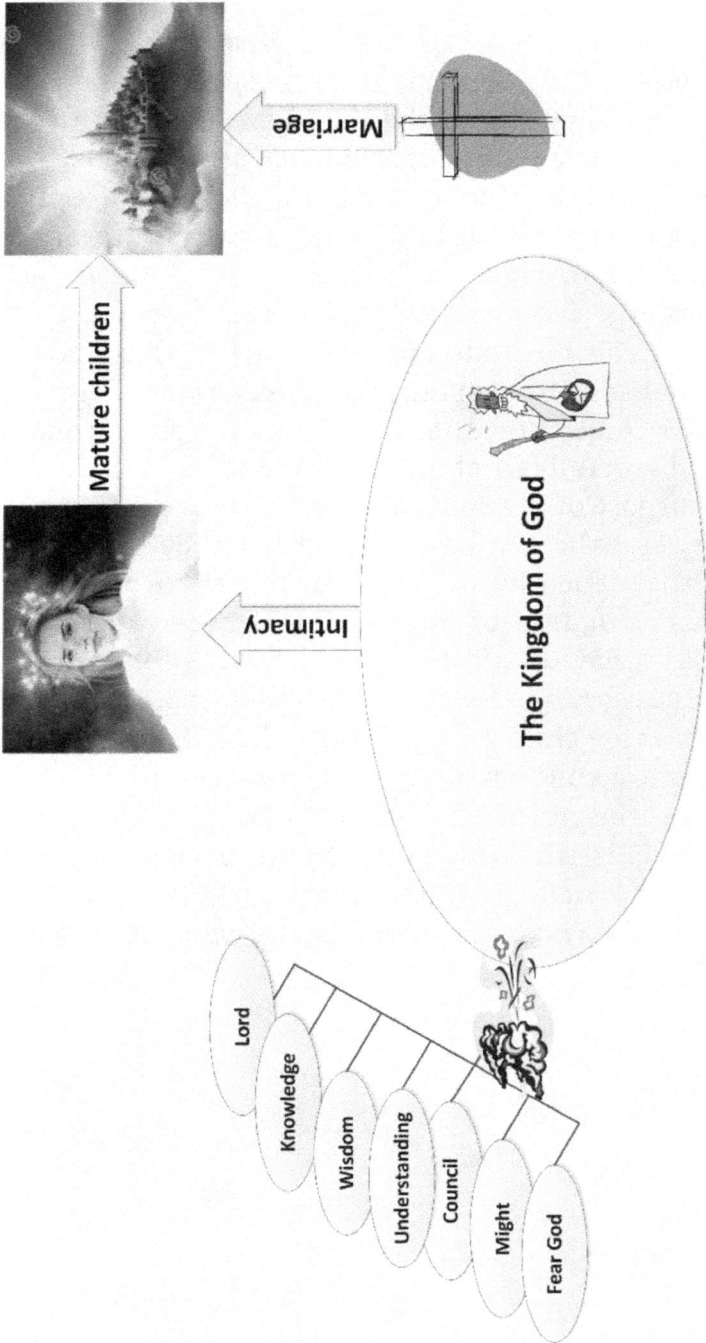

Marriage

Mature children

Intimacy

The Kingdom of God

Lord

Knowledge

Wisdom

Understanding

Council

Might

Fear God

What is important to realise here under this section discussing the Holy Spirit, is that the Spirit of God is essential in giving the qualities to the Kingdom of God – it is after all Spiritual. Scripture also says that God is the Father of Spirits. And we have to hold-up this picture above, and compare that to the Beast created through the carnal efforts of men. We could also for instance compare similarities between the two kingdoms e.g. carnal knowledge versus spiritual knowledge. Each of us can meditate and add more to these pictures and the comparisons to each other. The purpose of these pictures is purely to stimulate the thought process of opening our eyes and ears to what it is like, not unlike a parable.

The purpose of the Spirit of God is so that the Church (people of Israel and the Christian Church) can sit on the Kingdom of God that is led by the attributes of the Holy Spirit (using the visual language of Revelation). Between the Kingdom of God (the husband) and the Church (the wife) exists Spiritual communion, bearing forth a child – first Christ (as the first fruit), and then more children (as the first fruits). From the deeds of these mature children a city – the new Jerusalem – is born as depicted at the end of Revelation in Revelation 21. Also perhaps note that it is with this city – the new Jerusalem – that the bridegroom is married and becomes a Husband (see Revelation 21: 2 and 9) and not with the Church as we so often believe.

8 THE PEPPER

"And for this reason God will send them strong delusion, that they should believe the lie..." 2 Thessalonians 2: 11

John is very descriptive in Revelation describing three players namely Satan as the Dragon, the first Beast from the sea and the second Beast from the earth. In Ezekiel 28 whilst the Prophet laments over the king of Tyre, he references to Satan and the cause of the fall of Satan. Because of Satan's beauty he lifted his heart and rebelled against God and because of his splendour he corrupted God's wisdom in him. Reflect on Ezekiel 28: 12 – 15 and verse 17 NKJV:

""Son of man, take up a lamentation for the king of Tyre, and say to him, 'Thus says the Lord God: "You were the seal of perfection, Full of wisdom and perfect in beauty. You were in Eden, the garden of God; Every precious stone was your covering: The sardius, topaz, and diamond, Beryl, onyx, and jasper, Sapphire, turquoise, and emerald with gold. The workmanship of your timbrels and pipes was prepared for you on the day you were created. "You were the anointed cherub who covers; I established you; You were on the holy mountain of God; You walked back and forth in the midst of fiery stones. You were perfect in your ways from the day you were created, Till iniquity was found in you.

"Your heart was lifted up because of your beauty; You corrupted your wisdom for the sake of your splendor; I cast you to the ground, I laid you before kings, That they might gaze at you."

Ezekiel 28:12-15, 17 NKJV

We will now draw for ourselves a reflection of the Dragon (or Satan), the first and the second Beast as described by John in Revelation.

The Dragon

If you refer to Revelation 12, you undoubtedly wonder, "Why does John use the image of the Dragon? If it represents the Snake of old or the Satan, why not simply name it as such?" After creation, all creation was Holy, the heavenly creatures and the angels included. In Genesis 3: 1 (NIV) we encounter Satan for the first time:

"Now the serpent was more subtle than any beast of the field which the Lord God had made."

Image: In the time that Revelation was written, John depicted him not as a Serpent, but as a Dragon. It is evident that he has transformed his image from the time of being called a Serpent or the Devil or Satan. 2,000 years later, would he still look the same, and what image would he associate with himself? Let's choose a logical, symbolic image so that there can be no misunderstanding later.

GOD (the Dragon)

Name: In Revelation 17: 8 (KJV) John gives us a name: "The beast that thou sawest was, and is not; and shall ascend." John expressed that the Dragon (through his spirit) in John's day was called "I was what I was, was not, and will be what I will be". Does this sound familiar – not yet? Moving forward to our day, "I will be what I will be" translates into "I am what I am". Does *that* sound familiar? He is known for our purposes of Revelation and will be towards the end of days by the name God.

Shortly after the fall, we view another attack by Satan and his angels in the common area in Genesis 6: 1 to 7 (NIV):

> *"When human beings began to increase in number on the earth and daughters were born to them, the sons of God saw that the daughters of humans were beautiful, and they married any of them they chose. Then the Lord said, 'My Spirit will not contend with humans forever, for they are mortal; their days will be a hundred and twenty years.' The Nephilim were on the earth in those days—and also afterward—when the sons of God went to the daughters of humans and had children by them. They were the heroes of old, men of renown. The Lord saw how great the wickedness of the human race had become on the earth, and that*

every inclination of the thoughts of the human heart was only evil all the time. The Lord regretted that he had made human beings on the earth, and his heart was deeply troubled. So the Lord said, 'I will wipe from the face of the earth the human race I have created —and with them the animals, the birds and the creatures that move along the ground—for I regret that I have made them.'"

The Animal (Beast from the Sea)

Up to now, we have identified four of the role players. The fifth character in Revelation is the Beast from the Sea. It is interesting because the sea in Revelation could mean from the spiritual realm of or from amongst the sea of people. In other words this Beast has something to do with the spirit, either from the spiritual realm or a spirit from amongst all the peoples of the earth. We have previously considered the rising of this Beast from the sea and considered some of its carnal or fleshly traits. What we have to realise though is that there is a spirit that breathes within this Beast. Using our thesis that the harlot woman sits on this kingdom, then from their spiritual union children is born (meaning similar to God's righteous way first the person's soul is turned, then their heart grows in relationship and then their mind hardens in the renewed way of thinking). What we then observe in the later chapters in Revelation, chapter 17, that the scarlet or harlot woman sits on this Beast and from their offspring's actions and deeds the corrupt city Babylon as opposed to the picture of the new Jerusalem is born.

This spirit is "breathed" into this kingdom in Revelation 13: 2:

> *"...and the Dragon [Satan] gave him [the Beast] his power, and his seat, and great authority."*

Because there has been a declaration of war between two kingdoms, it is important that we possess a clear, concise image of the Beast – the deceiver – before we can draw this scenario. We choose the following:

Name: We see that the animal is powerful and from the deceiver. It enters an area where it is worshipped. In Revelation 17: 10 we see that the Animal has seven heads and the eight is the body:

> *"...And there are seven kings: five are fallen, and one is, and the other is not yet come; and when he cometh, he must continue a short space. And the beast that was, and is not, even he is the eighth, and is of the seven."*

Does this sound familiar: similar to the description of the Holy Spirit in the beginning of Revelation? This carnal animal with the spirit of seven previous dominating kingdoms heading it represents or mimic the Kingdom of God headed by the Holy Spirit.

Image: Removing the images from Revelation 13: 4 (remember, John used the images so as not to confuse his audience), the passage reads: "And they (the harlot Church) worshipped the dragon (false God) which gave power unto the beast (carnal kingdom led by spirits from seven previous dominating kingdoms): and they worshipped the beast (the carnal kingdom), saying, Who is like unto the beast (this carnal kingdom)? Who is able to make war with Him?"

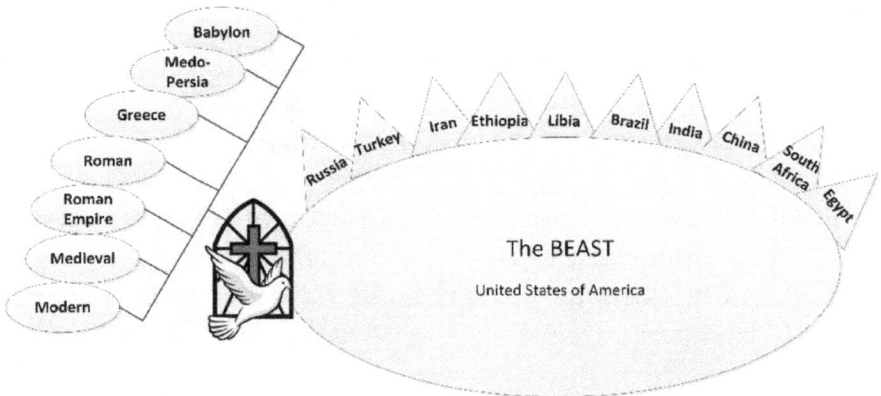

It is so tough to comprehend, is it not? The characteristics of the this beast are the following:
1. Deceit

2. Power

The other worldly aspects of knowledge, wisdom, power and riches (relationships, finances and health) will be given to the person praising and worshipping in this spirit, especially as the beast grows in strength.

The Anti-Christ (Beast from the Earth)

By now, it should be quite obvious to see where this is going – is it not? Revelation 13: 11 to 12 (KJV) articulates this:

"And I beheld another beast coming up out of the earth; and he had two horns like a lamb, and he spake as a dragon. And he exerciseth all the power of the first beast before him, and causeth the earth and them which dwell therein to worship the first beast, whose deadly wound was healed. And he doeth great wonders, so that he maketh fire come down from heaven on the earth in the sight of men, and deceiveth them that dwell on the earth by means of those miracles which he had power to do in the sight of the beast."

If it is not quite apparent, Satan will wield immense power. He will be allowed to deceive many as if he is in the image of God, through the counterfeit carnal kingdom (formed by seven spirits of previously dominating human kingdoms), and once fully manifest, will bring forth a king or a Christ-like figure for this carnal kingdom. The anti-Christ will rule his kingdom from his city Babylon. Note here that it will not be some person that is against Jesus Christ, but a person in the image of Christ... a false or deceitful Christ.

Hopefully, by now you are sitting upright. For the purpose of war, it is important that we call the enemy by the name he uses when attacking us – and that we have a clear and concise image of this person, of the deceiver. We choose the following:

Name: Christ.

Image: The likeness of Jesus Christ, but in a powerful state, possessing the same or even a greater display of power, as shown in the accompanying picture.

CHRIST (the anti-Christ)

Here we can see that Satan is intent to recreate with the assistance of human kingdoms what God the Father always intended namely a Spiritual Kingdom headed up by the seven Spirits of the Holy Spirit, whom through knowing the pure woman (the Church) bears mature children (in soul, heart and mind) whom then builds through their acts a city the New Jerusalem who is then given to Jesus Christ. Except here we see in the imitation version that it will be carnal, or a human effort, and not Spiritual in its nature. Therefore the number 6-6-6 in the spirt simply meaning that all three are through human effort, lacking the Holy Spirit. We can therefore consider that the 6-6-6 will have a meaning including:

- First 6: is a dominant human kingdom, that took its inspiration and lead from seven previous human kingdoms. The one seated on the throne of this kingdom and giving it its power and authority is Satan;

- Second 6: the impure woman sitting on this Beast is an un-Spiritual or false church or a church dominated by human inspiration, culture and communion with the Beast. It was initially given the role to be a representation of the sanctuary of God the Father here in Earth, but have not done so accurately. The mistake comes in with the understanding of the discipleship path to mature or that leads to perfected saints. In God the Father's eyes only a woman that was give the role of representing His sanctuary, can later be seen as a harlot if she misrepresents His purposes;

- Third 6: the children's, borne from the Beast and the harlot woman, deeds are responsible for the formation of the Babylon city in contrast to that of the intended New Jerusalem. This false city is given to the false-Lamb with the epicentre of his power seated in this city during a three-and-a-half year period of tribulation.

- The description of the ten horns on the Beast is given to us simply as a means to determine the timing and the maturity of this Beast and for us to recognise the accompanying and ensuing events.

The image of the 6-6-6 in contrast to the image of the 7-7-7 can therefore be given as follows:

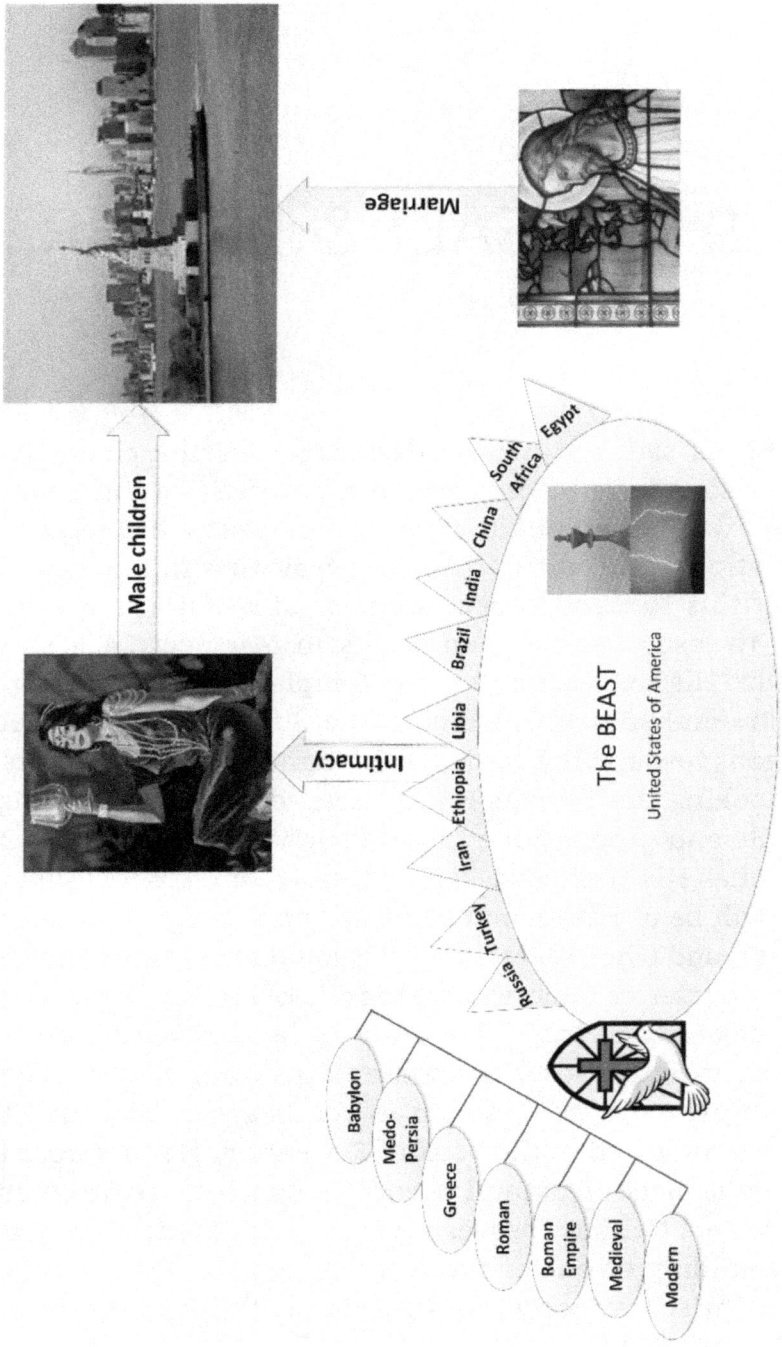

Marriage

Male children

Intimacy

Russia Turkey Iran Ethiopia Libia Brazil India China South Africa Egypt

The BEAST
United States of America

Babylon
Medo-Persia
Greece
Roman
Roman Empire
Medieval
Modern

9 THE SALT & PEPPER

This salt and pepper description of the characters all sounds very confusing. But hopefully in this chapter it will become quite clear and evident what the book of Revelation is all about. The best way to shine a clear light on all this salt and pepper stuff is gained by again referring back to Jesus Christ's own words in Matthew 24. Jesus just finished His last teachings in the Temple in Jerusalem before His capture and subsequent crucifixion. After leaving the Temple he heads towards the garden, the Mount of Olives, opposite and overlooking the Temple. He just settled down overlooking the Temple and prophesying the destruction of the Temple in 70 A.D. when His disciples asks Him to tell them "straight" what the sign will be of His second coming, and the sign for the end of the age, and when will this be. We could phrase it differently by asking ourselves today what is the one key thing that we can and must take as the central theme for the book of Revelation?

Note carefully Jesus' response. Jesus does not highlight by starting to talk about a sign in the heavens, of which there are two indicated in the book of Revelation. Neither does Jesus highlight facts of natural events of which there are many in Revelation. Neither does Jesus point to any events in heaven, or the sounding of one of the seven trumpets. Observe carefully Jesus Christ's response, because this is the key sign or signal of His imminent second coming or the end of the age, around which all of Revelation is built. Jesus answers this pivotal question with an express warning: "Take heed that no one deceives you". Specifically also note the audience He is saying this too – His own disciples! This is not a message to the world, or to other religions… this is a message for the Church. Note carefully therefore the pivotal event signifying the core to the question when can we expect Jesus and the end of the age. And the answer is it commences with a great period of deceit:

*"Take heed that no one **deceives you**. For many will come in My name, saying 'I am the Christ', and **will deceive many**"* Matthew 24: 4 and 5.

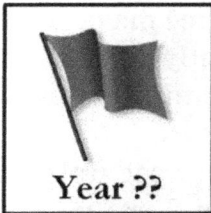

Year ?? Therefore the book of Revelation will not make sense to us, unless we identify this pivotal sign to look out for, namely the great deceit in the Church and everything that accompanies it. We will call it our "flag in the ground" event. And if we can place that, then we can place all the activities that build up to that event and also that follows this marked position. For the purpose of this book and to illustrate what the flow of events would mean in our lives, we will place a "flag". This "flag" or date can move, however, which I will demonstrate at the hand of three definite, and visible events, to be defined shortly. But irrespective of the three preceding events, our "flag" in the ground or date, signifies the coming of the anti-Christ (…the one saying I am the Christ) as described in Revelation. For the purpose of this book we cannot peg this "flag" to a specific date. What we can do however is highlight three events, of which two forms part of three "woe events" described in Revelation, that will precede and consequently determine this "flag" date. These three events will come suddenly upon especially the Church to prepare the disciples in the Church for the coming of the anti-Christ. And secondly, what we also know for sure is that Jesus Christ will come back a second time on the feast of Trumpets, following the time of the anti-Christ, the largest and only unfulfilled prophecy of the Old Testament feasts (typically between September and October) as per the Jewish calendar. That means then also the anti-Christ must appear during the feast of Trumpets, and after three and a half years be forcefully removed during the feast of Passover.

There are three woe-events described in Revelation. Two of these woe-events transpire before the appearance of the anti-Christ, and the third woe-event itself is the false one saying "I am the Christ". But carefully note that there are three major events, of which two are woe-events, that will imminently and suddenly come upon the Church prior to this "flagged" coming of the anti-Christ and include:

1. Revelation 9: 1 to 12 – the fifth trumpet unleashes locusts from the bottomless pit. This first woe-event is one of three last mercy events allowed by God to get the people in the Church prepared during a five month period. Those marked on the forehead by God, or perfected saints, will be unharmed during a period where people affected by this plague will cry out to die rather than endure the pain of the plague. These perfected saints through their witness of how they came to be perfected, will in turn lead many in the Church affected by the plague to become prepared similar to themselves due to their discipleship testimony during this time. During this period each individual's false Christian theology and our own understanding of Christian maturity will be laid bare for ourselves and also others to see. We can call it, if we like, a period where our own false adoption and understanding of Christianity stops giving us the answers we require and our circumstances prove to us and allow our mis-conceived Christian theologies to run out of answers. This period will be a merciful furnace

period where God will expose our own preparation weaknesses and remove these strongholds from our hearts, minds and lives. Those who adopt the witness of the perfected saints and submit to be discipled will be healed. It is a period that some would call a "great revival". Others would call it a period of great pain, a great plague, and become embittered towards God in this time and start moving towards a "great falling away".

2. Revelation 9: 13 to 21 – the sixth trumpet loosens the four Angels from the Euphrates unleashing the second woe-event killing a third of mankind. With fire (red), smoke (blue) and brimstone (yellow) a sudden event will come over the earth. This event is the second last mercy event allowed by God for people in the Church to prepare themselves and grow towards becoming a perfected saint. The duration of this event is not given to us in Revelation, but if I had to guess I suspect the duration of all these final three preparation events, prior to the appearance of the anti-Christ or the third woe-event itself, will probably be seven years - because that just sounds good and feels like a complete prophetic cycle. Minus the five months of the foregoing woe and the three and a half years of ministry of the two witnesses that follow it leaves us with mostly three years and one month for this tumultuous time where nearly one third of all people on the earth will succumb. We could muse as to whether this will be a natural disaster represented by volcanic eruption or a period of atrocious war that accompanies this period, but it is accompanied by fire, smoke and brimstone. One could reason that if war, it would be at the global scale between the current superpowers represented by the United States of America entering into unconventional warfare with the Peoples Republic of China – and fallout ensue. You can already read and see all the signs, in the

media, of that cooking pot potentially starting to boil over. However, if you zoom out a little and reconsider the chapter on the Beast and consider that China is at best one of the ten horns on the back of the Beast, potentially represented by the USA, and these Countries ultimately give their authority to the Beast... a world war as the cause of these deaths start making less sense. If the enemy kingdom to that of God is organising itself and ultimately unifying itself into one kingdom – a war amongst the members of the Beast start seeming less realistic – because a house divided against itself cannot stand. That would tend to lean us more toward volcanic eruption/s signifying the earth's ever increasing birth pangs as the time of the coming of Jesus Christ approaches post that of the anti-Christ.

3. Revelation 11: 1 to 14 – thereafter two witnesses appear on the scene and prophesy for a period of three and a half years to the Church. This is the final mercy event allowed by God for the people in the Church to build their figurative ark like Noah did. But unlike Noah who built a physical place of safety the saints are called to build a place of spiritual safety by growing themselves, their household and their congregations to perfected saints. You could probably guess that these two prophets will represent Moses (or fire, signifying the last leadership callings) and Elijah (or water, signifying last repentance baptisms).

If you are still confused, let us return to the salt and pepper analogy. Imagine you are standing at your present date of reading this chapter and looking forward into the future on your timeline. You are trying to look forward and at the same time looking up into the sky to see the second coming of Jesus Christ. This second coming of Jesus Christ is represented by a salt shaker and all the three persons involved that we portrayed earlier namely God the Father, Jesus Christ and the Holy Spirit.

But as you are piercing into the future, barely seeing this salt shaker coming down in the not too distant future, you are suddenly troubled and overtaken by three mercy-events that we described above. As you gather yourself after being overtaken by these events and continue to pierce into the future to spy the salt shaker, your view is filled and blurred by a pepper shaker coming down between yourself and the salt shaker. With the pepper shaker between you and the salt shaker, you suddenly cannot see the salt shaker and your entire view is taken up by the pepper shaker represented by the Dragon, the first Beast out of the sea (this human made and unified kingdom) and the second Beast (… or the one that identifies himself as "I am the Christ" and the king over the now unified Beast kingdom). Only when three and a half years have passed on your timeline can you again see the salt shaker coming down, with the pepper shaker now in your past. This analogy should give you a good description of the Revelation events, and also the warning of Christ that we perused at the start of this Chapter.

We can now therefore start building a timeline for ourselves, that probably makes out the core events that we can and should expect as the end of this age is drawing to a close. These events that we described can possibly be shown on a timescale that we can present as follows:

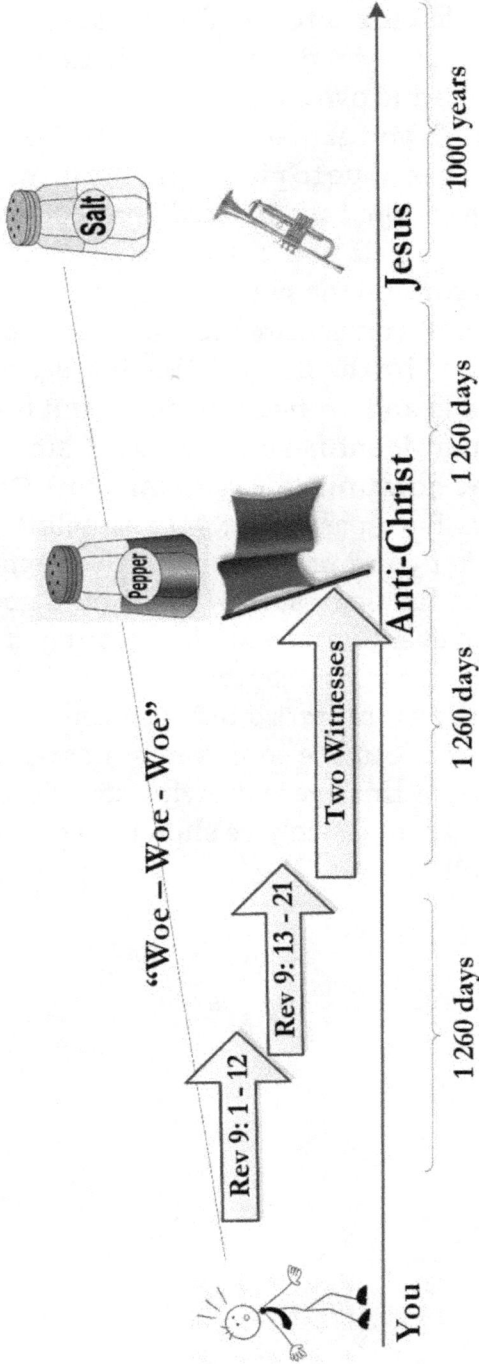

"Woe – Woe – Woe"

Rev 9: 1 - 12

Rev 9: 13 - 21

Two Witnesses

You

1 260 days

1 260 days

Anti-Christ

1 260 days

1 260 days

Jesus

1000 years

In this image we see ourselves standing looking forward into the future and looking forward and upward for the second coming of Jesus Christ, here represented by the salt shaker. As we gaze out, we are shaken by three mercy events separately described in Revelation 9: 1 – 12, then Revelation 9: 13 – 21 and finally in Revelation 12. These events are allowed to test us and assist us who are currently in the Church to prepare ourselves to become perfected saints. Our view of seeing the coming of Jesus is now blurred by a pepper shaker that is coming down in front or before the event of Jesus' coming. This pepper shaker event is a deception and will trick or deceit a very large percentage in the Church currently expecting the coming of Christ. During this time of deception the people in the Church will be given to the deception of their own understanding and they will be baptised in the name of the god, the kingdom (the spirit) and the one that calls himself "I am the Christ". This in the spiritual world replaces the 7 – 7 - 7 that a Christian is supposed to be marked with on his forehead and right hand during baptism and discipleship growth to a perfected saint (God's Spiritual knowledge, wisdom and understanding) versus man's own delusional and carnal knowledge, wisdom and understanding represented by 6 – 6 - 6. After three and a half years of this deception (the perfect time period to grow a Saint to perfected maturity in soul, heart and mind), we can now see the coming of Jesus Christ on the feast of trumpets. This coming however follows shortly after the removal of the anti-Christ, and is heralded in by cosmic events and a sudden appearance of Jesus Christ witnessed and audibly heard globally. Hopefully this image will assist us greatly when we read and interpret coming events and the book of Revelation.

10 THREE WOES

When initially reading and writing about the book of Revelation, my focus was always on the events, the deception, the description of the characters and how these events fitted into the rest of the Bible, what the bearing and relevance is on us today and many other themes. What was completely lacking was the heart of God our Father. God is always good, always merciful, always full of love, compassionate, full of patience, endurance and longsuffering. Yes, the curtain on this age will draw closed and must draw to a close. But even in the melting pot of the happenings of this event, it will all materialise according to God's will, and what deception and circumstances He will allow to be unleashed on us. The prophet Isaiah managed to summarize God's emotions and feeling so accurately towards the end of these times when he described God like a pregnant woman towards the end of her term, or a warrior that is psyched up and about to engage in war, jumping up and onto His throne saying – it is done! What is done… we might ask? And the answer is the time for the gentiles to repent, believe, be baptised, receive the holy spirit and grow to perfected saints. This all meant to be completed in a three-and-a-half year time period under a good management or discipleship programme and a willing disciple. This curtain will draw to a close. One could also say that this occurs when the number of the gentiles is full.

But in the lead up to this process, the Church will be full of people proclaiming to be God's sons and daughters. And God is about to run out of patience for them to come to maturity. God intends to send a deceiver, to herald in the culmination of all tribulations and with it accompanying deceit. The events in the run-up to the time of this deceiver and the deceitful time itself will test the heart of every Christian believer and their maturity towards becoming a perfected saint. But before this time of the anti-Christ, depicted by the Dragon, the Beast from the sea and the Beast from the earth, God will allow for three major and final events. The three events will firstly test the perfected state of every Christian, allow for each Christian to prepare and grow to perfection and finally allow for each one in the Church to make their final choices in their discipling and belief system. We can call it a time of mercy from God allowing each individual, household, and group of Christians to measure and adjust, if needed, on whether their building work will stand the test of time. We could also call it a time of great revival, or a time of great exploits for the Church as many unprepared Christians will be led to perfection. As the writer Bob Sorge recently posted: "Revival is when the Church repents". These last few years, marked by two of Revelation's "woe" events or rather three mercy events (if you include the ministry of the two witnesses) will suddenly wash over the Church, and allow people to make their final adjustments and preparations in their Christian maturity status. That is all before the anti-Christ appears on the scene.

We might argue that with clear tests during the three mercy events, time to repent of our "golden cow" customs in the Church, clear and instructive ministry and proclamation of the way to prepare toward Christian perfection will allow us to see a very high success rate of conversion and growth to Spiritual maturity. That would be our hope. But that is not what we see in Jesus' parables. Jesus in Matthew 25 starts with the parable of the wise and foolish virgins. Noteworthy is that He starts with the little word – "then". When is this "then" that Jesus is talking about we might ask ourselves? And the answer is during the preparation time throughout the three mercy events. And from the parable of the five wise virgins and the five foolish virgins we gather that the preparation statistics during God's final mercy period is not great within the Church. Yes, it will be a great time of preparation and revival of Christians taking the opportunity to grow to perfection. But alas we see that roughly only fifty percent of Christians in the Church choose to prepare themselves wisely. If we take 2 500 million Christians in the Church, it is a great revival period if fifty percent choose to grow to full maturity within this final seven year window allowed for by God's mercy. But fifty percent choose not to from the parable, and that is a gigantic number of Christians that choose to remain foolish and face the deceiver without adequate preparations. If we look at statistics alone it has little impact. But if Scripture talks about brother against brother, and father against son, and mother against daughter it starts sinking in. Next time when you go to Church and sit down for the service, look around and notice that every second person you observe will choose against the perfected saints during the period of the anti-Christ. Now that starts hitting home if we consider the sheer amount of Christians that will turn against Jesus. And that is after the final mercy event where one of the prophets namely Elijah will purposefully come to return the hearts of the fathers to the sons, meaning unity in the faith between brothers will be proclaimed and returned. But we could agree that more or less 1 250 million Christians opting out of these final preparation callings is extremely high and sorrowful do you not think?

The three final mercy events, before the third woe-event culminating with the coming of the false Christ, will come onto the Church suddenly because it is allowed for directly by the hand of God. It will however not catch God or His chosen leaders unaware. God will have been making preparations for these years well in advance before these ensuing events, by raising leaders for His people. You can read authors such as Dr David Pawson's *"Normal Christian Birth"* or Bob Sorge's *"Secrets of the Secret Place"*, *"Fire of delayed answers"* or *"Pain, perplexity and promotion*" and you will start noticing that God has been quite busy setting up authority for times such as the final three mercy events. Allow me to give you my own personal experience of this. Whilst I was writing my first version of *"Revelation, the end of times?" by Hoffman Prinsloo*, which I must self-confess was not my greatest attempt at writing, I contemplated much whether it was only notes to myself or whether it had greater meaning to a wider audience. I finally decided to publish the work, but did not inform many people of it. The very same day, I was relaxing that evening in a bubble bath, God gave me a picture as I was lying there that started to form a vision of how things will fit together in the end times. It was a picture of a wide river, of rushing waters and accelerating as in a flood. As the waters rushed past an island on the left, God was standing on the fiery island fishing. He had a fishing rod and caught a leader far on the opposite side of the river far from the island. As He reeled the person in from the cold and rushing waters, the fire from His fiery presence on the island cleansed this person as he was drawn near. It was a tumultuous affair for the individual as this fire caused him to lose all his principle relationships, finances and health (we can call these all our "riches"). But with that he was drawn onto the island and into the very presence of God the Father. This fire he experienced in the process of being drawn closer to God sanctified him and set him up to lead others in times of acceleration and similar tribulation. Not a far distance downstream from this fiery island was another triangular island that split the rushing waters of the river into a narrow stream to the left and the majority of the waters rushing past to the right hand side of the island. The stream to the left represented sheep selected by Jesus Christ Himself standing on this island represented by blood, water and Spirit, and goats that simply passed by on the right side of the island. This vision or picture is very much presented by the following depiction below. The fire on the island represents individual leaders that is being drawn closer in a fiery process to God the Father in preparation of tumultuous times to come. We could say it represents a type of a Moses spirit of leadership. The island downstream represents repentance in the blood of Jesus Christ, baptism in water and growth in the Holy Spirit to a maturity of perfected saints. We could say a type of Elijah spirit of leadership. The noticeable fact for us should be that there are authorities that has already written or writing books on these matters of normal Christian birth or others on leadership selection through personal trials and tribulation. In other words, we might not be that perceptive as the Church on these matters, but it does not prevent God from working unbeknownst to us, setting processes in place including literature, individual leaders and especially events that will bring about an unexpected "suddenness" to it all. We are therefore asked over and over in Scripture to be wide awake in these times, and start to observe these processes.

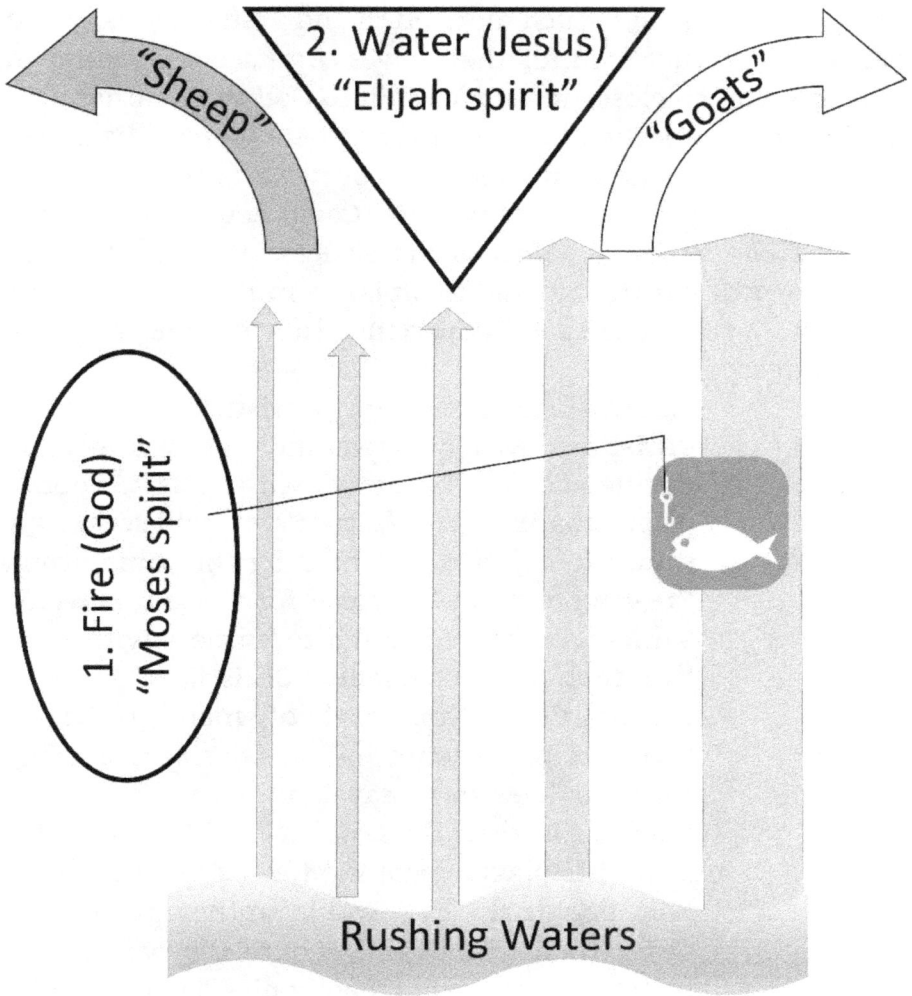

2. Water (Jesus)
"Elijah spirit"

"Sheep"

"Goats"

1. Fire (God)
"Moses spirit"

Rushing Waters

People are looking for all kinds of signs and events that will herald in the final times. But this is a fruitless exercise, because it will come suddenly upon us. We should be keeping watch for the Revelation 9: 1 to 12 event that will wash over us in the Church. People phoned me during the advent of the Covid outbreak and asked me if this could be a sign of Revelation, especially the accompanying inoculation as a sign of the Beast. I firstly want to respond by saying that I wish people would start reading and studying their Bibles much more often and preferably daily and get their spiritual food for themselves. And secondly enter in and come much closer in relationship to God their Father on a daily basis that Jesus Christ paid for so dearly with His blood. That way we will not be swayed about by news, false statements, false word, rumours and conjecture. Covid could have been a shadow of things to come as far as Revelation 9: 1 to 12 is concerned. But the five months plague in Revelation differs completely from our Covid experience in a number of ways, including:

- Mature and immature Christians and non-Christians was affected and got sick equally during Covid. Whereas with this 5-month plague mature or perfected Saints will seemingly miraculously be unharmed by the same event. Creating a major platform for these unaffected Saints within the Church to witness with their lives to their affected fellow-Christians.
- During Covid you read of many physician accounts of patients in intensive-care begging for their lives to be saved as the infection was plucking at their lives. But with this prophesied 5-month plague people affected by the event will beg that they would rather be put to death than to live and endure the pain of the infection tormenting their bodies. That is a major difference.
- And unlike with Covid if a Christian then repents and follows in the way of maturing as a Christian toward perfection the plague would miraculously fall away from them. There was no such luck or many such testimonies during Covid.

Once the first of these "woes" are finished the two other events will follow similarly suddenly during which time Christians will gain greatly by repenting and starting to walk in a way towards becoming perfected Saints. We therefore have a 5-month plague, a third of mankind dying and then two witnesses not unlike Moses and Elijah witnessing to Christians to repent and mature toward perfected saints in order not to fall for the later deception of the coming anti-Christ. But alas, more than half of the Christians in the Church navigate through these three "mercy" events choosing not to prepare themselves, their households and Christian communities for the coming deception. And then God Himself finally relents and gives them over to the deception of the anti-Christ or rather to the one calling himself "I am the Christ". One could now contemplate and even ask oneself – is God the Father then unjust or unfair to allow the deception of the anti-Christ to be released on these Christians? Or in other words must His patience, endurance and long-suffering continue eternally... or at some stage come to finality? Hopefully we will all come to see and hear and understand that God the Father is only good, and full of mercy and patient beyond our understanding during these times that ensue.

11 PERFECTED SAINTS

*"I am the Lord your God. And is
no other. My people shall never
be put to shame." Joel 2: 27b*

When Jesus Christ witnessed of the end-time events He paralleled it with the times of Noah. Now in Noah's day there were probably at least three generations that were informed of the ensuing events namely:

- Enoch, Noah's great-great grandfather is documented as heaving walked so close to God that he was taken up alive in heaven... not dissimilar to Elijah. Now for a man in those days living only for 364 years was practically unheard of, especially for a man walking so close to God. And one cannot but ponder on what information God shared with Enoch on ensuing catastrophic events and how preparation must be made to escape the circumstances.
- Methuselah, the grandfather of Noah is where you really start observing God's mercy towards the preparation of the ark for Noah and the future generation of this family to escape. We can be certain Enoch from age 64 starts ministering to Methusaleh on what is to come. And we then see that Methusaleh only passes away on the day the tribulation of the flood

commences, becoming the oldest man at 968 years of age. The mercy of God extending beyond anything ever experienced by then man, to ensure ample time for Noah to complete his preparations to construct the ark. Perhaps we should see that the same 7-7-7 that each perfected Christian is marked with, in the Spirit, on the forehead and right hand is symbolic and similar here at the end of this Church dispensation than Noah having had to build a vessel.

Isn't the above amazing? In those Patriarchal days all four these generations, if you include Noah, were staying in the same place or camp area, and would live in each other's direct vicinity sharing common meals around the campfire. Therefore Noah would have been told that his great-grandfather was taken up alive, would have seen Methusaleh live to become the oldest person in history to facilitate that his preparations are complete. He also experienced that his own father passed away on a significant number of years 7-7-7. And all these pointing Noah to the fact that God is full of mercy, and intricately concerned and speaking into Noah's preparations to continue... extending mercy, upon mercy, upon more mercy until the preparations were finally complete. And then the great flood came.

You cannot but see the mercy of God extended to Noah's family in the years leading up to the flood. And therefore when we talk about "as in the days of Noah" the first thing that we must see is that similar to those days God the Father will extend mercy, upon mercy, upon mercy to the Christians in the Church to get their house in order. Note however that Methusaleh and Lamech had many other children, but also note that only Noah took heed and prepared – it is the strangest thing isn't it if you meditate on how from the same group of people with the same set of circumstances and input/teaching they choose different outcomes? Another important thing to take from the days of Noah, is that it was the unprepared that were plucked away by the ensuing circumstances, but Noah and his household who prepared were saved. And when we read in the New Testament that like in the days of Noah two persons in the same field, one will be plucked away and the other remain... please do not make the mistake, like many do, that the one plucked away is being raptured. No, to the contrary that person is plucked away to the grave by the ensuing circumstances. And the one that is prepared is saved and remains – much like in the days of Noah. We have to start opening our spiritual eyes and ears to this – as per the parable of the wheat and the tars that Jesus foretold of the end-days. The tars are gathered and burned, before the harvest of the perfected Saints can ensue. We therefore have much to glean from the comparison to the likeness to the days of Noah, and apply it to our days.

It should by now be top of mind that we ask ourselves: "So, how do we in these days, like in the days of Noah, build for ourselves, our household and our Christian community an Arc – like in the days of Noah"? And the answer lies in becoming spiritually mature as perfected Saints. But before we consider what that could possibly look like... we have to ask ourselves what is God the Father's motivation behind all of this. What is driving a good, patient, enduring, long-suffering, loving and merciful Father to send a deceiver to the Church? It just does not feel right – or does it?

The motivation behind God the Father's actions is that He wants to show His glory. And always immediately after hearing that most of us forms the wrong picture in our minds of what that entails. And to understand that we have to go back to word of "first mention" of the explanation behind what the glory of God in this world, or land of the living if you like, looks like. And we find it in Exodus 33: 18 to 19 when Moses asks God – please show me Your glory. Now, we have to sit upright and have our eyes and ears wide open to the ensuing answer – otherwise we miss God's heart in all the Revelation events. God cannot show His full glory in the Earth, it is way beyond what this place can take, and that is why Moses cannot look at it head on. Even if Moses met with God face-to-face numerous times before and after this event, here he cannot face the fulness of

God's glory in a full frontal experience – it is way too big. But what ensues is interesting, with Moses being allowed to face God's full glory that is meant for him personally only once it has passed. And we can or might as well as proverbially decipher that here by paraphrasing: "Moses, although My glory is way too big to manifest in this earth, it will however manifest through you Moses, with your own eyes seeing the goodness of God in the land of the living, your own ears hearing the name of God proclaimed before you wherever you go, you receiving My grace (later Paul states it as God's mercy) in your life and receiving My compassion in your life with an abundant increase in your "riches" which include relationships, finances and health".

In other words God wants to show to the World His goodness and glory through the lives of perfected individuals, households and Church communities. In order that the World is desirous and converted to come into relationship with God through the Church. But, as we can instinctively see, hear and feel instead of the Church influencing the World through the glory of God manifesting through individual Christians and Christian communities, the reverse is actually true. And because the Church is starting to lose its mandate to disciple individuals and communities to come into perfection... God now has to intervene, for the sake of all the people He loves. The Church is increasingly representing Him poorly and His intended glory through the individuals and Church communities. And it is leading the World astray. This is indeed a very hard word to swallow. What then does it look like when the Church implements God's vision we might ask?

Without any veil or mincing our words, it looks like Paul's vision for the Church given to us in Ephesians. Giving clarity to the full Spiritual meaning of it, it should hypothetically look like what follows. Jesus Christ when He ascended into heaven gave gifts to the leaders of the church. These leaders in turn must use their gifts to train saints sitting in the Church benches to lead up various ministries in their Church. These Saints, not the leaders, must minister to every adult person entering the community to achieve Christlikeness ideally within a three-and-a-half-year process of discipleship redeeming their soul, then their heart, then their mind to become and walk as perfected Saints. Until each one entering the community of Saints has reached this level of maturity in order for the body to be able to edify itself in love. All of this in order for the glory of God to manifest through the lives of the individuals and the Christian community into the worldly community where they were placed. This in turn will lead people outside the community of Christians to want to join and become part of this fulness.

To shine even more light onto the meaning of perfected saints we need to set up a measuring tool for our Churches using the following insights of how we get to perfection and what perfection looks like. Imagine a diagram. At the very beginning of it is a Church. The horizontal access is time measuring the age of an individual or a community. This horizontal axis represents a life in the flesh. That is how we are naturally inclined to measure. We say that a person is 50 years old, or that person has come to Church for 30 years. And it somehow has meaning to us. God the Father on the other hand measures on the vertical access of our imaginary diagram, and this Spiritual access has only four measuring points and include: infant, young man, father and perfection. You can be 50 years old and have been in Church for 30 years... but quite possibly not even birthed in the Spiritual measure of God. We are not going to go into too much detail here on the spiritual steps of infancy, young man, father or even perfection, we can refer to "*Christian Unity: Walking in a Motivating Climate*" by Hoffman Prinsloo to cast more definition on this. But in summary through well-structured leadership each Saint with a willing faculty should ideally be grown through a three-and-a-half year process to a perfected Saint. Commencing with repentance, believing in Christ Jesus, baptism in water and baptism in the Holy Spirit each Christian achieves the first phase of infancy. Then through discipleship grow into young men through spending personal time with God the Father every morning. Then finally as they spiritually grow on a forward and exponential upward curve all their "riches" formerly consisting of fleshly relationships, finances and health will be stretched and die in a process of a wilderness of fiery trial or walk. Successfully walking through these fiery trials the Saint reaches perfection, where their riches of relationships, finances and health are restored manifold through the glory of God manifesting through them. They then bear forward rising daily and walk in perfection. This walk is evidenced by humility, childlikeness, mercy and compassion.

And what does this way of walking daily in perfection further look like, we ask ourselves? It pretty much resembles a see-saw that one used to see in children's play parks. It is a balancing beam pivoted in the centre by a hinge namely faith. If kids played on it and you placed an equally weighted child on each end, they each in turn kicked off the ground to rise themselves in turn high into the air. Then with the other side reaching the ground, equally kicked of sending the other child hurtling back to the ground. And the secret of it all was the balance. If you placed an overweight boy at one end, and a skinny girl at the other, the whole game would be negated with the skinny girl high in the air and the weighty boy wedged to the ground. And the intention of the see-saw would be rendered use-less. Now with this image in mind when Christ is asked by His disciples "increase our faith" or Paul is later years asked "how must we walk" in both instances the image of the see-saw should conjure up the answer in the mind of a perfected Saint. Now with his soul already redeemed, his heart redeemed and his mind redeemed, he is called to daily walk a life of sacrifice and offering. In terms of the see-saw picture a perfected Saint should have perfect and equal balance between sacrifice toward God on the one end and offering toward his fellow Christian brothers and sisters on the other. If we had to expand the sacrifice-side toward God, as Paul and the Apostles also wrote, it consists of only two aspects. And these are walking in holiness and purity towards God your Father day-by-day with your body, eyes, ears and senses. And this is developed over time as we each work it out for ourselves spending time with Him every day in the secret place. Secondly permanent thanksgiving with our mouth and tongue to Him on a daily basis. It would include thanking Him, praise and worship and honouring and glorifying Him with our lips. The catch however is that these traits represent pure water in the Spirit reaching the shores of heaven. And therefore our same lips and tongue cannot now spew out salt water by talking and saying anything dis-honouring about firstly our brothers and sisters in the Christian community. It equally compels us to honour all men in the World with our words. That is a tough one, but we are called to honour other people with our lips and tongue. Irrespective of what they have done to us, are doing to us or plan to do to us. If we cannot find one thing honourable to say about another person, then we should rather push our thoughts and feelings down within in us – and not utter dis-honourable words. Because if we want the fresh water from our thanksgiving to reach God's ear, we should not permit any sewage or brackish water to roll of our tongues and pass over the opening of our lips dishonouring people.

On the other side of the see-saw balancing the daily sacrifice towards God our Father we find serving diligently in our Christian community. It means that as a perfected Saint if we expect our faith to grow or expect God to bless us with riches, we must offer up our time, our talents and our treasures (yes even our finances) to our Christian community where we serve. That means that we cannot simply sit with our bums on the church benches Sunday after Sunday. It simultaneously mean that our leaders must empower, facilitate and trust us to serve and minister, but equally we must become willing and trustworthy to take this upon ourselves to serve. Diligently means more regularly than not. Using our little discipline that we have been given, to form the habit of regularly serving. Serving means you can pour tea for all you care, or you can do healing ministry if that is your thing, you can prophecy if that is your inclination, but perpetual service and regular service is what keeps the balance.

You can see some of us are good and feel comfortable at only spending time sacrificing to God our Father spending personal time with Him, even doing so on a daily basis. Some others again are only active in the Christian community serving with their time, talents and treasure. But if these are not equally balanced on a daily, weekly and monthly basis, all our efforts and good works attain to nothing – zero. It should be equally sacrifice and offering. Jesus said we only grow our faith by working, that is tilling the soil, planting, watering, pruning and harvesting amongst our brothers and sisters. And equally resting by entering into the secret place with God our Father through our daily sacrifices to Him. In that way we come to be known as perfected Saints, and open the sluice gates of heaven for the outpouring of God's glory in and through our lives.

If we take this above description of what individual Christians, our households and our Christian Community should look like and be active with as the measuring rule – few of us will argue that this is not what we or our Churches represent. Yes we have programs upon programs, we are busy, we have our own interpretations... but one thing is for sure we are not consistently producing perfected Saints and definitely not within a focused three-and-a-half year discipleship period – are we? And that is what God the Father wants so that He can manifest His glory in the Earth. And that is why the time or window of the Church as we know it is coming to an end with a great shaking through trials and tribulation. These type of events produce only two outcomes amongst Christians namely – perfected Saints on the one hand, and a great falling away on the other. This would usher in a new dispensation where Jesus Christ Himself will return to rule with an "iron sceptre" or accurately represent where Adam & Eve, Israel and the Church failed to epitomise God the Father's sanctuary in Heaven.

12 THE RAPTURE

The book of Revelation talks about a time when Christ returns and we are "caught up in heaven". However the word rapture entered into our modern theologies. And it is not the task here to analyse how this theology came to especially the United States of America and thereafter influenced the rest of the World. The question here to consider is whether there will be a rapture, or a taking away of the Saints, whereby the Saints miss all the trials and tribulations that is seemingly and obviously busy coming over this World of ours.

Will we still be here when the five month plague of Revelation 9 is released, or during the time when the two witnesses of Revelation walks the earth, or will we miss the three-and-a-half year time of the anti-Christ which call himself "I am the Christ"? Looking at the mainstream online video streams it seems as if the promise is that the Saints will eminently be raptured into heaven and need not be concerned with conditions deteriorating much further on the Earth. It seems that many Churches are similarly preparing their Saints to prepare for the eminent rapture to heaven... in order to escape their obvious deteriorating environment. The question is what should we believe and take as our own? Perhaps Dr David Pawson put it best in a conversation during a conference in the United States of America. He said that it is perhaps the best for a Saint to prepare themself as if they have to walk through the worst trial and tribulation in the history of mankind. If they are then raptured, it is a convenient escape from this reality. Alternatively if they have to remain and walk through this trying period – at least they are prepared. But if you contemplate a little it would be terrible to expect an easy outcome but then, with an unprepared mind, have to walk through such a testing time. Wouldn't that be similar to sending soldiers into war without any basic training and expect them to flourish in the war?

If we leave all the social media, internet and populist beliefs behind us and only focus on Scripture, it does not seem feasible that the Saints will be raptured. And that is simply because of numerous texts that point to the Saints having to endure the deceit, the trying times, the persecution and the challenge of enduring these times described in the book of Revelation. On the one hand if you take all the Bible texts and parables of Jesus Christ into consideration the balance of probability points to the Saints being present through the tribulation period.

However, there does seem to be a number of exceptions that we have to consider. These include the male child, the 144 000 male saints, of Revelation 12 being taken away to heaven at an early stage. Then there is also a taking up or gathering into heaven of the Saints as Christ appears. If we meditate on it the Saints seem to be gone during the thousand year rule of Christ, or little is said about them. Only the 144 000 male saints and the saints decapitated during the tribulation period are mentioned and return to rule with Christ for this period. There does therefore seem to be quite a bit of "traffic" taken into heaven, and returning from heaven to rule, and taken up to heaven to miss the millennial rule of Christ. It depends on what bus your ticket is booked – don't you think? Let's look at the separate events and ponder on those a little as they appear in the book of Revelation.

We read of one hundred and forty-four thousand male servants that are sealed in Revelation chapter seven for the first time. And it seems that they are of the tribes of the children Israel. And from Revelation 7 verse 3 and 4 we see that this is before the four angels that is granted to harm the earth and the sea is given liberty to do their task. If we read further, we see these same four angels now in Revelation 9 verse 13 with the sounding of the sixth trumpet, allowed to unleash the second "woe" event namely to kill one third of mankind with fire, smoke and brimstone (or sulphur). It is therefore implied that these male servants are sealed on their foreheads (they become perfected saints) before this event is allowed to occur. We now encounter the same 144 000, who will rule with Jesus Christ during His 1000-year rule with an iron sceptre, in Revelation 12. We see a star sign heralding in these times. The male child that the woman is with in heaven in Revelation 12 are these same 144 000 perfected saints. We know this because our beast from the sea in this star sign is now fully mature with its body, seven heads and ten horns ready to devour this "male child" of 144 000. This 144 000 strong first "child" is meant to rule the Nations with a rod of iron. In other words the Church delivers these 144 000 male perfected saints – the discipleship system has been established to deliver these perfected saints. The matured world government with its accompanying religious system will threaten to extinguish these servants – because it poses a real governmental threat to the beast from the sea. And we see these 144 000 men taken away to heaven, only to return later with Jesus Christ for His utopian rule. Are they raptured we might ask? And the answer in Revelation 12 verse 5 is that they are "caught up to God and His throne". If our interpretation of this event is summarized by the word rapture... then yes, they are raptured. More interesting though is to meditate on what these men will do, experience and be trained in for a few years in heaven, before they return to rule with Christ.

We now know that 144 000 men are taken up early and prepared to return to rule with Christ. But what about the rest of us we might question ourselves? If the message in this book is correct, then the deceitful time of the anti-Christ sent specifically over the Church, will produce only two types of Christians. The one half will become embittered towards God the Father, curse Him, accept the anti-Christ sent to rule in the

Church, and become part of the great falling away. The other half will hold onto God the Father through Jesus Christ and await His return, and become perfected saints in the process. If you are lucky and decapitated, not a pleasant thought, during the period of rule of the anti-Christ then you also can return to rule when Jesus Christ returns for His millennial rule.

We also see two witnesses that appear in Revelation 11. These two gentlemen after a three and a half year ministry is killed by the anti-Christ or the beast that ascends out of the bottomless pit. After a number of days of lying exposed in the streets however, new life is breathed into them and they are resurrected. Immediately thereafter they are caught up to heaven, and we do not hear of them or see them again in Revelation.

For the rest of the Saints already sleeping, or living through the three-and-a-half year period of the anti-Christ there seems to be a different outcome. And this is based on a few logical assumptions. The first being that only the 144 000 saints we looked at earlier and the decapitated Saints from the three-and-a-half year tribulation period seem to return and rule with Jesus Christ. The question now begs to be asked, where is the rest of us. We can track our progress by considering Scriptures that state that when Jesus Christ appears those sleeping and those still living are caught up to Him in the heavens as He appears and is coming down towards the earth. We are transformed in an instant and given new bodies. However, we are not mentioned as ruling with Jesus Christ during His millennial rule. The question begs therefore whether we are then here or taken away after receiving our new bodies? This picture painted in the parable of the wheat and the tars suggest that the wheat is "gathered" after the tars are destroyed. That after the kingdom of the beast and the anti-Christ is destroyed and Satan imprisoned… in other words the tars are harvested from the earth… the harvest or taking of the saints commence and are completed. We simply cannot say whether these Saints are now also "caught up to the throne of heaven" or whether they return with Christ to continue living on Earth during the millennial rule period. But we are not told much of them in Revelation after they are gathered to Christ in the air as Christ comes down to rule. And we only read of them again at the final judgement seat of God as He rolls-up this earth and this heaven as we know it.

We can see therefore that there is quite a bit of traffic going up to heaven and coming down from heaven during the time period that the book of Revelation covers. Perhaps a small time diagram helps to give us a clearer picture that we can meditate on:

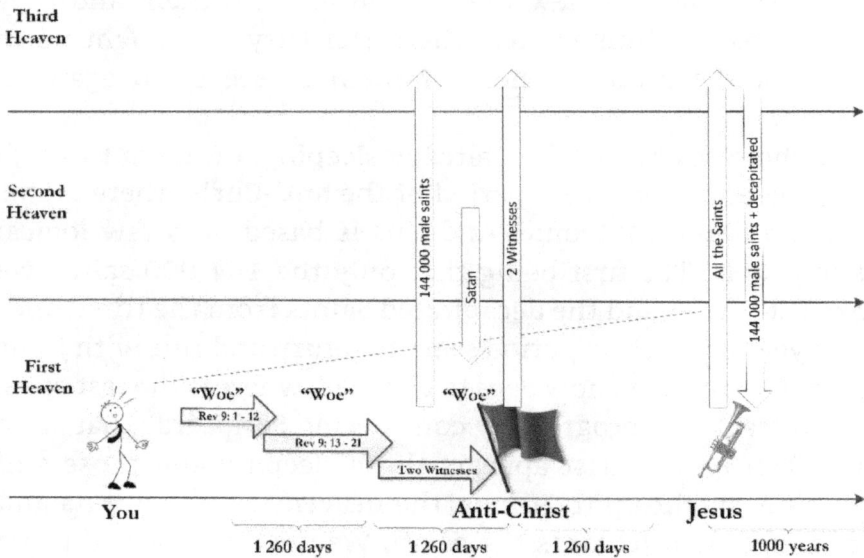

What this diagram communicates is that as we stand from where we are now, looking forward and upwards. We can expect three events to overtake us on the earth with specific bearing on the Church for its preparation for the eminent coming of the anti-Christ, before Jesus Christ can return. These events include a 5-month plague, a third of human kind killed by fire, smoke and sulphur and two witnesses bringing a message of repentance and discipleship to the Church. These three events, used by God the Father, are meant for the Church to adjust and start cultivating or discipling perfected saints. The world government, or the beast from the sea represented by the body with seven heads that ruled historically and now with ten distinct new horns or countries growing off-of it, an integral part of the body of the beast, becomes fully visible. It threatens to kill the first male child of the woman now in labour to bring forth the 144 000 perfected saints – future rulers with Christ. We see these taken up into heaven to God the Father's throne. We then see Satan thrown onto the earth from heaven where he is currently ruling. The time of the anti-Christ commences lasting for a period of three and a half years. At the onset of this period the two witnesses are killed, resurrected and taken up into the heaven. We then see Jesus descending and all the sleeping and living Saints caught up to Him in our skies, or first heaven, and we are transformed in an instant. Only the 144 000 male saints taken up and the saints decapitated during the three and a half year period of the anti-Christ returns to the earth with Christ to rule with an iron sceptre. And during this dispensation of Christ's millennial rule many, many, many people whom are currently not Christian is affected by the true representation of the sons and daughters of God the Father and converted to become Christian – a mandate that partially failed during the Church time, era or period.

13 THE CHURCHES

*"Also I gave you cleanness of teeth
in all your cities, And lack of bread
in all your places; Yet you have
not returned to Me" Amos 4: 6*

The book of Revelation commences in chapters 2 and 3 to address seven churches. It continues in Revelation 11 verse 1 and 2 where John describes how he is given a reed like a measuring rod and instructed to measure the temple of God, the altar and those who worship there. But he is also instructed to leave out the court which is outside the temple and not to measure it, because it has been given to the gentiles.

This message is key to understanding what the book of Revelation is all about. It is a message meant for the Church and all that worship there, and not a message for the people outside the Church. And that is the tough part for the Church and Christians worshipping there to take in. Because we tend to orientate ourselves to think that we as Christians are living good lives, and the world is on a daily basis going more astray. Surely we might think that we are righteous and if anything God's judgement will commence with the people living in the world and not with the Church and the Christians serving there, right? But that is not what the book of Revelation prophesies and neither what Scripture has to say about that. In fact the opposite is true... God our Father says that His judgement will commence with His own people, in other words the Church and all Christians serving there, before His judgement will at a later stage turn to the world. This is key to the understanding of Revelation. The focus on the events, the mercy events, the measuring, the deceit sent by God Himself, and ultimately the judgement in the book of Revelation is all focused on the Church, much like light from the sun is concentrated through a magnifying glass onto a small concentrated area only.

Therefore do not read the book of Revelation and look at the world expecting the people in it to be judged. Rather we should read it and look at the Church and the lives of Christians and start asking ourselves why God the Father need to or ultimately find it necessary to judge us? If we do not fathom this early on in the reading of these prophesies, we will become confused on why certain people seem to come through the revelation events fairly unharmed. As a case in point consider that there are literally hundreds of millions of people and multiple kings and kingdoms that suddenly get spoken of and exist during the millennial rule of Jesus Christ here on the earth. Now, assume that during the time of the great deception of the anti-Christ the Church is divided straight down the middle. On the one side a great falling away of Saints and on the other those that continue to serve God the Father. And that when Jesus Christ returns, all those in the Church not serving God the Father through our Lord Jesus Christ is slaughtered... Seemingly however hundreds of millions of non-Church going people are spoken of during the millennial rule of Jesus. Therefore we can surmise that the book of Revelation speaks of the Church and the deceit that will be sent to it, to divide the Saints and cause a great falling away with the people in the Church accepting, being baptised in, and growing through the anti-Christ in relationship with a false god. And that on the return of Jesus Christ, these false Church goers, the government of the beast from the sea and the anti-Christ will be destroyed or harvested from the earth if you wish to use Revelation language. We see then the first two creatures thrown into hell at the end of that period namely the beast from the earth, or the governmental system of men, and the anti-Christ. Even Satan is not judged yet, but given a 1000-year sentence of being bound under the earth, to be released later for one last act of deception.

We therefore see that the book of Revelation is meant for the people in the Church. Warning them of events that will overtake us, deception that will challenge us and wrong choices during these times that will set us up for Jesus Christ's judgement on His return to rule. And that other non-Christian religions and even non-religious people, will surely be affected by some of the global events, but will otherwise walk away and continue through to Jesus Christ's millennial rule fairly unscathed. The focus as we started in Revelation 2 and 3 and Revelation 11: 1 and 2 is therefore purely on the Christian Churches and how it measures up. Our question should therefore start turning towards what is the rule of measure. Because surely that measuring reed, like any measuring instrument is calibrated against something? What does God the Father want or expect of us, that we are not doing as the Christian Churches, but represents His standard.

If we had to look at our Churches today the one observation is that the programs of the Churches are very busy. From sermons, praise and worship, conferences, courses etc. In business language it could be said that our Churches are extremely efficient – or doing many things. But are we effective – doing the right things right? To understand the rule of measure we have to understand God's heart for the functioning and operation of the Church. In laymen's terms what God wants is for the Christian Church to be so effective that within a three-and-a-half-year cycle the Church can take a new entrant and deliver them as a perfected Saint. We measure on a horizontal access in time or in carnal years, whereas God the Father only measure on the vertical access, namely Spiritual growth from being born as an infant, to growing into a young man, to becoming a father in the things of the Spirit, and ultimately onto walking daily as a perfected Saint. Imagine a picture of the individual Christian walking on a higher Spiritual path, with legalism or religion at the bottom of the slope to his left and license to sin at the bottom to his right. A picture that was aptly drawn by Dr David Pawson in his analysis of the book of Galatians and shown here:

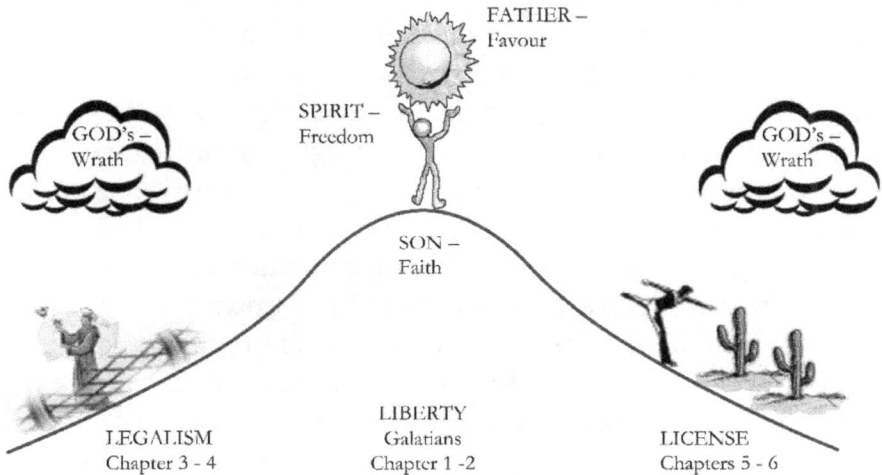

FATHER – Favour

SPIRIT – Freedom

GOD's – Wrath

GOD's – Wrath

SON – Faith

LIBERTY
Galatians
Chapter 1 -2

LEGALISM
Chapter 3 - 4

LICENSE
Chapters 5 - 6

Now walking on this path imagine that you, as you are taking daily footsteps forward in this way of righteousness, are balancing on a see-saw. On the one side you have what we would call sacrifices toward your Father. These daily sacrifices consists firstly of starting your morning walking in holiness and purity towards your Father with your entire body, including eyes and ears. Each person can work that out daily, but it is walking in the liberty of the Holy Spirit but with sin not an option. And secondly to be in constant thanksgiving with your tongue. Meaning thanking Him and praise and worshipping Him, honouring and glorifying Him. The more difficult part is to not ruin this fresh water proceeding from your tongue and lips with brackish water by dis-honouring a brother or sister in your Christian community, or any other person that comes across your path on any day. Now to balance the daily sacrifices to God your Father on the one hand of the tilting board, on the other side is offering. And this offering is done by serving diligently in your Christian community. It does not matter whether you are good at pouring coffee, or healing ministry, or prophetic words of exaltation to others, or teaching with your valuable time, your treasure including money and your gifted talent must be given diligently – meaning regularly or habitually. That is how a perfected Saint keep their daily and weekly life in equilibrium, and grows exponentially in their faith. The over emphasis on either sacrificial living or servanthood offering tilts and unbalances the see-saw causing the Saint to slip down the mountain and sin in the area of either legalism or license. This in turn causes the Saint to stop growing. That is until they climb back up the side of the mountain on to this way of wisdom through repentance. Then continue this balanced walking and growing in their faith stepping forward and upward.

The graphic depiction of what the agenda or focus for each Christian Church leadership and individual in this Church's community should be is shown in the accompanying diagram:

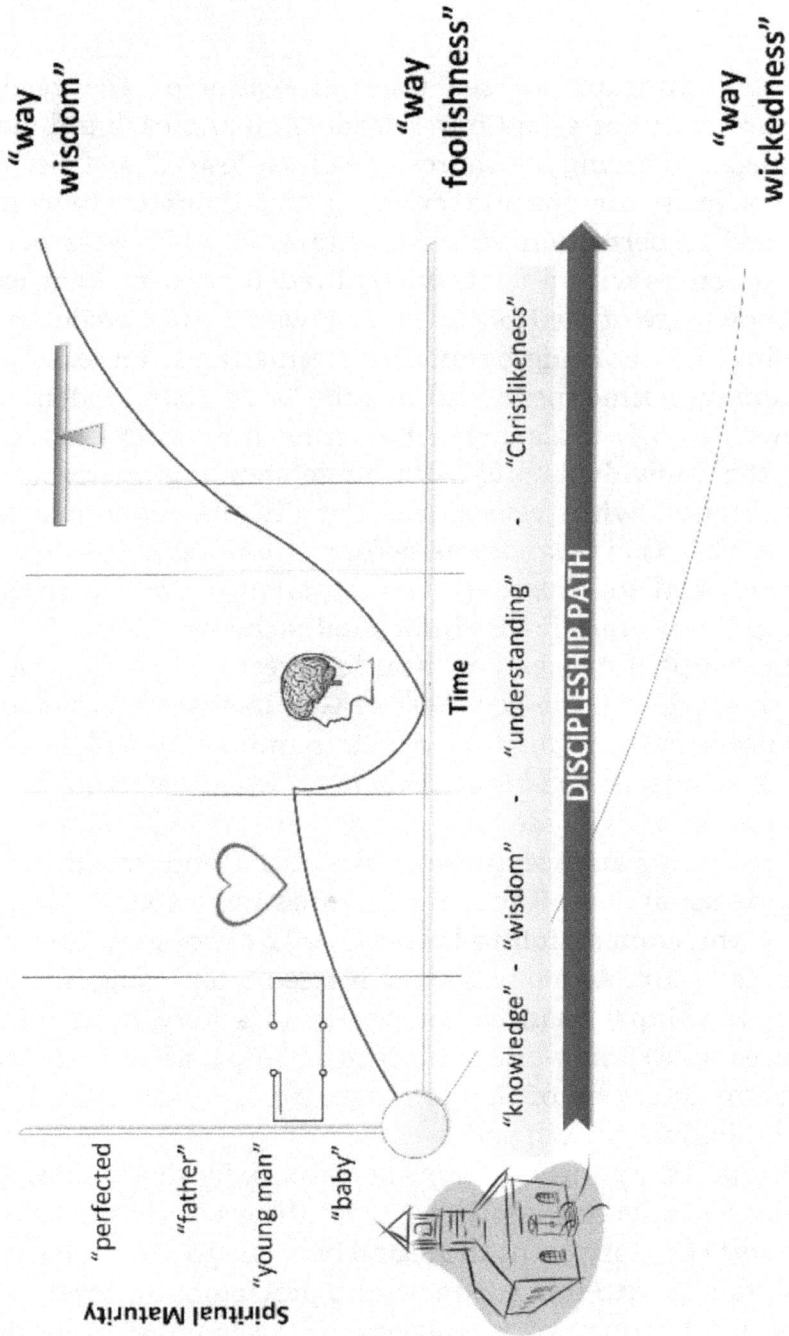

"way wisdom"

"way foolishness"

"way wickedness"

"Christlikeness"

Time

DISCIPLESHIP PATH

"knowledge" - "wisdom" - "understanding" -

"perfected"

"father"

"young man"

"baby"

Spiritual Maturity

In the diagram we see God's measure, or the reed to measure with, for each Church leadership and each individual congregant entering the Church. Ideally, as Jesus Christ discipled His disciples, any person entering the Community can be discipled to perfection within a three-and-a-half year period. It commences with a focus on soul redemption or increase in the knowledge of the Holy Spirt. Followed by heart redemption growing in morning-by-morning time and increasing in wisdom with time spent with God the Father. Mind redemption follows through trials and tribulations allowed by the Father into the individuals life with understanding increasing in identification with Jesus Christ. Finally the individual after feeling that God's hand was before, behind and beside them preventing their progress, now experience God's own hand lifting them up. If the individual achieves that all their relationships, finances and health is restored in the Spirit – and they will see the goodness of God in their circumstances and hear the proclamation of His name going before them. In the words of the New Testament when referring to Job, the individual will see that it was always God's plan if they endure with patience through the trials and tribulation in their personal lives. It was always God's intention to show His mercy and compassion to them in their restoration towards a perfected saint. As Job was more blessed after losing his riches of relationships, finances and health in a fiery trial, after he endured for a short while in his relationship with God his Father – it is the intention of God to similarly bless each Christian on this individual growth path.

Through the perfected Saints and especially also their diligent service towards one another, it was always God's intention to manifest His glory for us to see and hear His goodness. But more importantly with this goodness and proclamation of His name before us, the intention was always to draw in more people living in the flesh to subscribe and enter into the same discipleship path to learn to live in the Spirit. Because the Church is failing in its mandate to grow individuals to participate in such mature service in their Church communities, a true reflection of the goodness of God the Father, the last place that any person in the world wants to be is in some Churches - it simply does not reflect the glory of God in the lives of its Saints. And as Paul prophesied nearly 2000 years ago, the Church is therefore without visible power of the Holy Spirit. Yes, we hear thousands of sermons and praise and teachings but we simply do not see the power often or any longer. And that is because individuals in the Community is not raised into ministry leadership positions in the Churches. But that will return at the end of days, as the discipleship of Saints is sharpened again to reach perfection, and the words of Jesus Christ is fulfilled that we will do greater visible and audible works than He has done. In order to achieve that God will have to allow for three major mercy events to wash over the Church... allowing each to measure their discipleship doctrine and whether they are giving God what He wants – namely perfected saints.

At the end of this age, the Spiritual age, we will see two distinctly opposing Women or Churches riding on two distinctly opposing Beasts or Governments. The first will be the pure or Spiritual Church riding on the kingdom of God. And the other will be the harlot or man-made Church riding on the unified kingdom of men. The distinction will be that the Spiritual Church will increasingly mature individual Christians to perfection to themselves minister (preaching, teaching, healing, prophesying, worshipping, serving) to the body of the saints. Whereas the man-made Church will continue to see individual persons, priests, pastors, ministers, prophets and persons standing as God's representative on the earth, with their congregation remaining immature spiritually. Leaders of Churches facilitating the Spiritual growth of their congregants to serve through ministry will be the distinctively recognisable Spirit between the two Woman.

14 MERCY VS JUDGEMENT

"So you shall know that I am the
Lord your God, Dwelling in Zion
My holy mountain" Joel 3: 17

We established earlier that the Book of Revelation is written for Church going Christians, and not for the general public . With that established we also considered that Revelation shows God's judgement always starts with His own people and only thereafter move to the surrounding communities. We now have to determine for ourselves with which set of glasses we wish to read the book of Revelation for ourselves as a Christian. Is it principally a book of judgement, or a book predominantly showing God's mercy? If we read it as primarily showing God's judgement, which can easily be accomplished if you consider all the actions accompanying the breaking of the seals, the trumpet sounding and the bowl judgements. However if primarily reading it through the glasses of judgement we will miss God's heart message in the book of Revelation. And we will now try and colour in some of those mercy considerations for ourselves.

If we consider for ourselves that the current dispensation of the Church is drawing to a close, then the next dispensation heralding in the millennial rule of Jesus Christ is about to dawn. It should then not come as a surprise that the readiness of the Church will have to be established. And therefore we see the angel in Revelation 11: 1 and 2 handing John the reed like a measuring rod to measure. As in the days of Noah knowing that there is a great storm approaching in the form of Satan being allowed to bring great deception in the Church accompanied by great trials and tribulation, the question about the readiness of the Saints arises. It is then here we see God's mercy. With the knowledge that the deceiver will soon be unleashed, God timeously allows for three "mercy" events to test our theologies, beliefs and faith over a seven year process. We earlier considered these three events in the form of a five month plague in Revelation 9 verse 1, the death of a third of mankind in Revelation 9 verse 13 and finally the message accompanying the two witnesses in Revelation 11. And each time, and with each event the ability of the Church to produce perfected Saints will be questioned. If successful, the Saints will easily pass through that circumstance. But if their discipleship is found to be lacking the event will show or highlight our shortcomings. If we, the Church, repent and fix the errors in our understanding we can ready ourselves during any of the events, and within the seven years. Therefore over and over and over again we see God sending events and witnesses during those events that will minister the truth to us – how to be discipled onto perfection or godliness or Christlikeness.

However, we now have to consider whether it is the lack of God's mercy, rather than our hardened hearts that prevent us from repentance of the error of our ways. Or is it our teaching or own doctrine that has crept into the Church preventing us from correcting our preparations. Because in all three these mercy events we see that those with the seal on their foreheads, namely 7-7-7 walking as perfected saints, are spared from the ensuing event. During these events these perfected Christians will stand out, and be a witness ministering to their brothers and sisters.

However we see multiple times in Revelation 9 verse 20 and 21 the words "... did not repent". Even after the events testing us we observe with the two final witnesses, that will bring a very direct warning and message to the Churches to disciple onto perfection, the parable of Jesus Christ of the wise and unwise bridesmaids inform us that the probability of correcting our teaching and adherence to an effective discipleship path will at best be effective for only 50% of Christians. We can then question ourselves after seven years whether it is a lack of mercy on the side of God our Father that finally sees Christians overtaken by the deceit of Satan in the Church or our own stiff-neckedness. But more importantly we can meditate for ourselves on the possible reasons why Church leaders remain unwilling to teach a clear and effective discipleship strategy that leads to perfection. Or if there is then a clear leadership strategy why congregants choose and will choose not to follow such a path. We could possibly discuss several motivations for an individual congregant wilfully choosing not doing so. But ultimately we see that at least 50%, if not more, of Church leaders and congregants alike ignore all the danger signs showing them that their theologies are lacking and fall short of the glory intended by God. These are then overtaken by the deceit of the anti-Christ, which then during a three-and-a-half year discipleship path mature them in soul, heart and mind with the marking of 6-6-6 on their foreheads and right hand. It is only after a seven year preparation period and three-and-a-half year anti-Christ rule that we then see the judgement of Jesus Christ over these that fall-away.

Interesting enough we do not see God the Father's judgement over the people of the world at this stage. Only the false Christians are judged, and that judgement is executed by Jesus Christ. It is only at the end of Jesus Christ's millennial rule that we see God's judgement over the rest of the people that did not convert to and mature in Christianity. And with an iron fist, meaning with no error in leadership doctrines, we can be certain that many, many, many people in the world will convert to God the Father through Jesus Christ during the dispensation of His millennial rule.

Only after this one thousand year period of Christ's direct rule do we then see God the Father's judgement. This explanation should bring God's judgement versus God's mercy during the book of Revelation's events into sharp contrast for us. Even considering Satan we do not see final judgement or sentence to hell before the thousand year period of Jesus Christ is completed. Except for the anti-Christ and the beast from the sea (that represent human governmental systems) is sentenced to hell when Christ returns, but further than that no one else. It is only at the end of the millennial rule, after Satan has been bound for an entire thousand years, that God returns. That after Satan again deceives humankind. Then only do we finally see God the Father's judgement. And it is with these mercy, upon mercy, upon multiple mercy eyes that we have to read the book of Revelation – especially from the perspective of the Church. We are not currently living in a period of judgement as the Church but in an era of mercy. That is until God returns for final judgement after Christ's millennial rule.

15 THE TIMELINE

With the first attempt and first publication of the Revelation: The end of Times? I observed first-hand how dangerous it is to give or even hint at any specific date. In the first attempt, trying to make it relevant to a current reader, it stated that the "flag in the ground" event is the date of the coming of the anti-Christ. Indicating that as soon as this date is determined, you can arrange the rest of the Revelation verses in accordance to this most important date. This first version indicated that this "flag in the ground" event can move – however used 2018 as an illustration date to plant this flag-event. Off-course only this date then cemented into the minds of all the readers – completely missing the point of the illustration.

In this version it is perhaps prudent to state that the "flag in the ground" remains the most important date – especially when referencing Jesus Christ's warning in Matthew 24. And that all the events in Revelation either lead up to this "flag in the ground" or follows on from this date. If we then empirically, use knowledge, wisdom and understanding given to us by God our Father we can colour in or build for ourselves a logical picture of what we can expect. If our flag in the ground represents the coming of the anti-Christ, the next question we can colour in for ourselves is more or less when we can expect him? And we can say to ourselves that the false Christ will definitely appear on the feast of trumpets, between September and October of any given year during the Jewish calendar event of feast of tabernacles. Why can we argue that? Because firstly Jesus Christ started His ministry on the Feast of Tabernacles when He first read during the Feast from the book of Isaiah, closed the Book in the Synagogue and declared – "today this word is fulfilled". And secondly we know today that the largest and unfulfilled of the three Jewish festivals including the feast of unleavened bread, the feast of weeks and the feast of tabernacles, the latter is the largest and unfulfilled prophecy. And this major date reflects the second coming of Jesus Christ. Therefore if we take into account that the time period allowed the anti-Christ is three-and-a-half years, we can firstly establish for ourselves that the anti-Christ will appear to the world and more specifically the Church during the Feast of Tabernacles of any given year, and again fall away on the Feast of Unleavened bread three and a half years later. It pretty much emulates Jesus Christ's first coming and ministry... but with a large amount of visible power and supremacy ruling over Nations. We can start with a visual picture as follows:

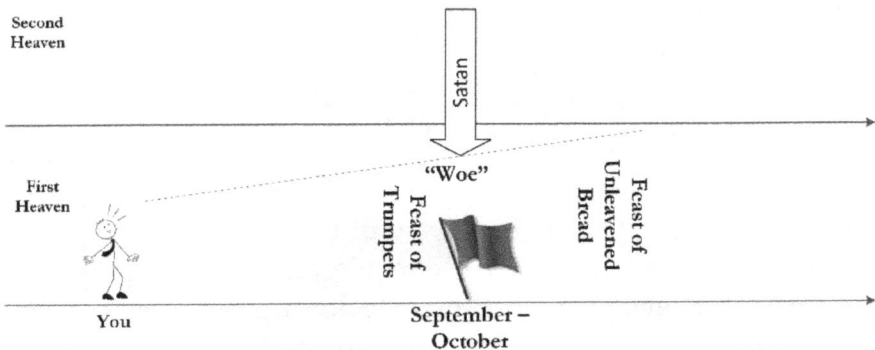

With this picture established in our minds, we can move towards the seven year period preceding this period of the third "woe" describing the anti-Christ. And this seven year period is probably the key period for us as Christians today. That is because the three events during this preceding seven year period will communicate beyond a shadow of a doubt to us as Christians that we should conclude our preparations. We

previously considered the events under the heading The Woe
Events, which shows a mercy period where God the Father
grants us time to see and hear if our theologies stack-up to what
He deems to be a perfected Saint. The three events are shown
in Revelation 9: 1 to 12 with a 5-month plague, Revelation 9:
13 to 21 where a third of mankind is killed by fire, smoke and
sulphur (and we can choose to think of it as either a world war or
probably our preference, if we consider what and who represent
the beast from the earth, rather volcanic action). These are two
"woe" events. And finally the two witnesses representing a spirit
of fire for Christian leadership, or a Moses-spirit, and a spirit of
water for Christian baptism, or an Elijah-spirit. Graphically we
can depict this as follows:

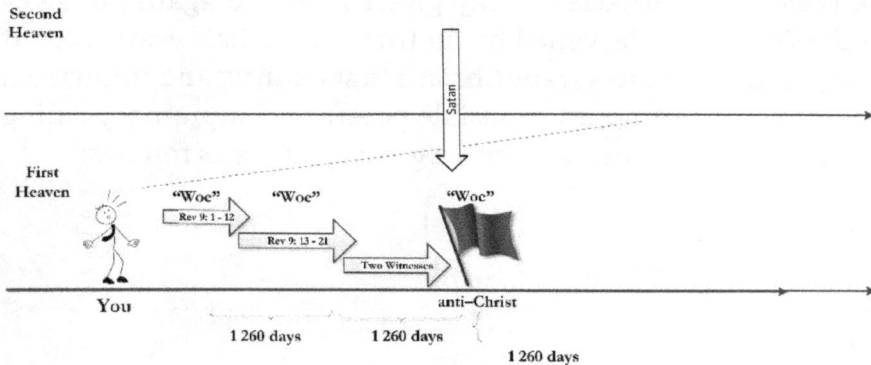

If we zoom out even further we will then see the build-up of
the beast from the sea which we considered earlier. This beast is
represented by seven heads of historic dominant kingdoms that
used to rule commencing with Babylon, Mede & Persia, Greece,
Roman Empire etc. The body of the beast is the eight that was
formed or rather preceded by the seven – and we contemplated
that this could in all probability be represented by todays United
States of America as the ultimate and current dominant world
power. We then see how ten kingdoms form on the back of the
beast in the last period leading up to the coming of the anti-
Christ. The anti-Christ then rule during the time of this beast
from the earth. We contemplated that at least the first five

kingdoms already prophesied by Daniel is represented by Russia, Turkey, Iran, Ethiopia and Libya. And we can and certainly should scan past, present and future news and economic news where these five parties are represented. But then we can already see through the BRICS formation it is starting to colour in the horns on the body of the beast from the sea, further represented probably by Brazil, India, China, South Africa, and possibly something like an Egypt if we had to guess. There are a number of issues that we should contemplate when we consider for ourselves the signs of this formation of the final ten Countries. Firstly, that in spite of all our news, economic indicators and feelings, these ten horns that are allowed to rule in the last days are only horns on the body of the beast. The body of the beast ultimately remains the largest of the entire creature, and ultimately somehow in control of economic, financial, political and military systems. We can muse at the central role a city such as New York as an example could play controlling world systems whether economic, financial, political, cultural, safety and security etc. That the Suni Muslem Countries represent the "young lions" in Biblical prophecy and ultimately complain when Israel is plundered.

When Jesus Christ ascended into heaven, the beginning of Revelation describes a scene where Jesus is the only one that can take a scroll from the hand of God His Father (refer to Revelation 5). Imagine that the names of the gentile Saints are written in this scroll, and sealed with seven seals. In order for Jesus to get the names of this inheritance given to Him, He has to break the seven seals as early as possible to open the scroll and to access the names. Therefore on this same date Jesus commences breaking the first seals. At that stage, some two thousand years back, imagine the beast from the sea already had five and a half of its heads already well formed. That simply means that in terms of current economic, financial, political, religious and other systems the beast is then already well on track to form this dominant system under which the world will ultimately have to bow. If left unchecked for some two thousand years this earthly kingdom would have been massively dominant by now. With this picture in mind, the first four seals broken by Jesus Christ two thousand years ago is to introduce flaws into the system, to ultimately set it up for a great fall. The first seal broken, Revelation 6: 1 to 2 already commences ever increasing victories for Satan in the area of the Church. And ever increasing from that date religion becomes the enemy of Spiritual growth and effective discipleship in the Church. Similarly the second seal broken commences with peace ever increasingly being taken out of the world to stunt the growth of the beast from the sea. The financial and economic system of the ultimate beast was increasingly stymied in larger and larger waves of scarcity commencing already two thousand years ago. And the introduction of increasing death on the earth through violence, food scarcity, sickness, animal attacks, war and death ever increasing from two thousand years ago. And we see that from the Kingdom of Heaven the forces of evil is loosed increasingly to keep back the progress of the this consolidated earthly kingdom. If this was not allowed this beast, the creation of men, would have been a monster by now. We see therefore that from where we are currently standing that the seven seals of the scroll were already broken some two thousand years ago. And that these events, voices and accompanying attacks on the kingdom of the earth, or the beast from the sea, has been growing in waves year-on-year. The picture in our mind has therefore grown to include the events that precede us where we are standing peering into the future:

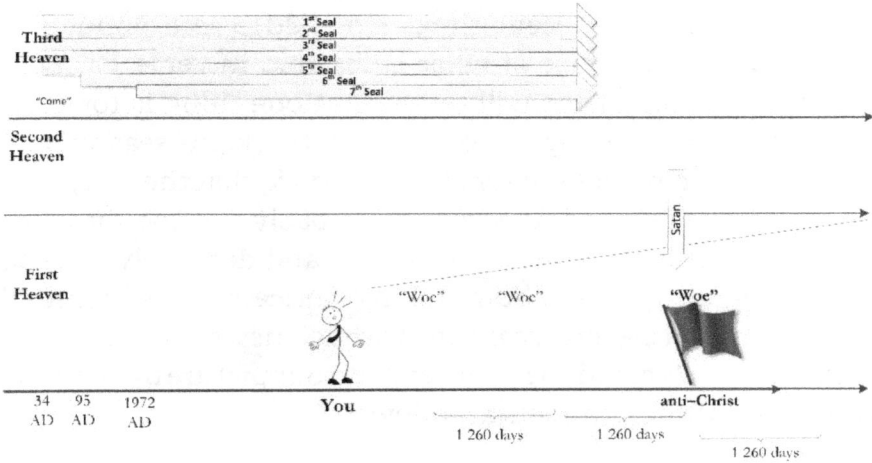

To give us a feeling for the trumpets that are blown in the Book of Revelation from where we are standing, we can return to 2015 when I published the first version of Revelation: The end of Times? At that stage in the beginning of the year 2015 whilst doing internet searches for raging fires destroying vast tracts of land – my searches came up mostly empty. Knowing that the first trumpet would see one third of trees and grass burned up, my searches yielded very little. But as we all know today, if you search any news or the internet for natural fire disasters you would end up with news of California, China, Spain, the Amazon, Greece, or almost globally you will find an increasing incidence of these fires. It does not take a genius to listen to conversations, reading news, or searching the internet to know that weather patterns have changed, the earth is warming and over population and pollution has accompanied the sounding of trumpets in Revelation 8: 7 to 11. And the only question we have to ask ourselves is what would our experience be and whether the fourth trumpet of Revelation 8: 12 has already sounded or is that still to come? Indicating that a third of the sun, a third of the moon, and a third of the stars will be affected with the sounding of this trumpet – does that literally mean that we will experience it as such. Or does that mean the blood moons, meteorite showers, and sun anomalies that we experienced a record number of in recent times since 2015 is a prelude to an increasing experience of what is foretold in verse 12? Let's wait and see... only time will tell us. But one thing is for sure, interpreting from the vegetation already struck, the seas already struck and fresh potable water already struck, that the woe, woe, woe events we referred to earlier is probably not too far away from our doorstep. And that we slowly and decisively have to start sitting upright and start taking notice of these foretold events – through cleverly scanning through news, conversations and searches. We could therefore expand our picture by showing the blowing of the trumpets as follows:

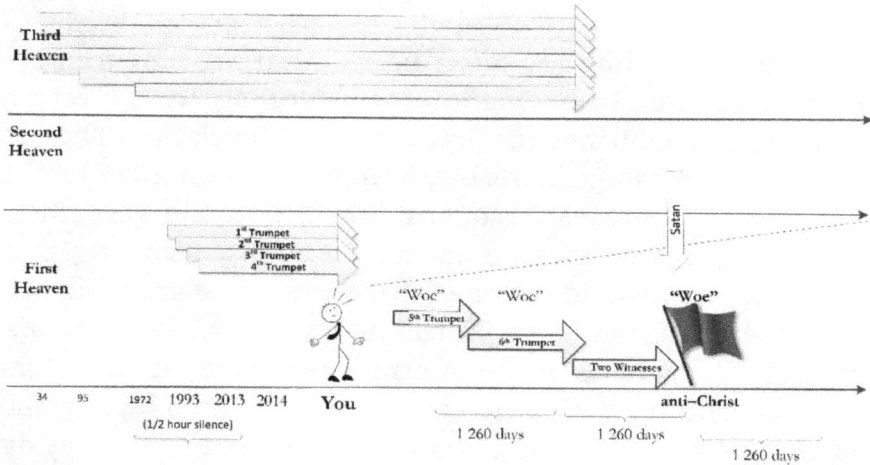

Before we continue to look at the events that follow the appearance of the anti-Christ, it should be evident from the previous picture that our focus as Christians, and the emphasis of this Book, must slowly start turning to Revelation 9 and Revelation 11. If these events are suddenly allowed to overtake the Church, how will we as leaders and congregants alike utilize a seven year period to disciple effectively to grow each congregant toward a perfected saint?

At the end of the ministry of the two witnesses we see that war is raged against Satan in heaven. Satan loses this battle and is thrown out of heaven. And whilst celebrations erupt in heaven, a quick glance to towards earth shows that there will be trouble on the earth for a short period. Satan himself is now prowling on the earth. And partnered with the full picture of the beast, namely with its seven heads, body and ten horns, it brings forth the beast from the earth – the one that calls himself "I am Christ". We have to try and picture for ourselves this unified governmental beast, with a woman riding on its back, through who's offspring a city Babylon is formed. And the anti-Christ is given this rule from this city as religious leader or head of the woman. The abomination is now complete in the eyes of God as Satan is seated as king in this fleshly unified kingdom, with a Church compromising to align with a unified government, and its off-spring or disciples aligning to the will of men and human standards. And a false Christ ruling from a human made city as head of the Church. Being baptised in the name of these, the number 6-6-6, will represent Satan's kingdom, a Church led by the power of men, and a false Christ receiving the authority over the Church and ruling from a human made city. A large percentage of people in the Church will give in to this deception. We will notice that not too long into the rule of the anti-Christ, the ten horns or Nations on the beast turn against and start destroying the very same adulterous woman or Church riding on the beast. These Nations, we can imagine each with its own historical reasons, always hated the Church – and the proverbial house divided against itself starts imploding. These ten horns always hated this woman, the Church, that is riding on this beast of the sea. Revelation says that God the Father always purposed it that way. Then in Revelation 15: 1 we notice another sign in the heavens. And here in Revelation 15: 2 to 4 we get a small insight into the condition of the perfected saints during this tribulation period – as if they are standing on a sea of glass mingled with fire, and victorious over the beast, over his image and over his mark and over the number of his name. They have harps of God in their hands, and we find them singing the song of the Lamb. Then we see the seven bowls of plagues as per Revelation 16 poured out over the kingdom of the beast, and all the men that have the mark of the beast and those who worshipped its image. The impact of the bowls is of a global scale and aimed at destroying this kingdom of the beast from the sea and the anti-Christ. Even in this process of these bowls being poured out, note specifically Revelation 16: verse 9 and again verse 11, that time is again given and allowed for these men to repent, but still they choose not to turn to God the Father through Jesus Christ. This period as we look forward is then depicted by our last sketch:

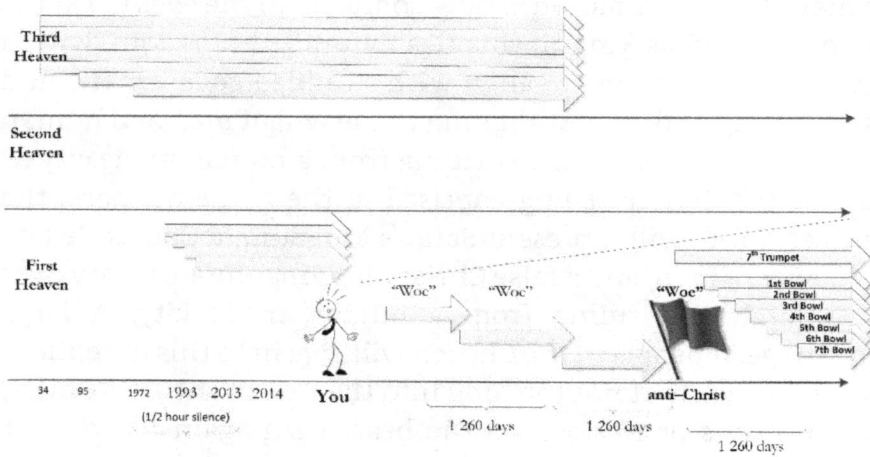

From the time that the anti-Christ commences his reign to its destruction seems short-lived, and on paper lasting only three-and-a-half years. But it is not that short if you think of it in terms of the trials and tribulation that Christians will have to endure during this period. The emotions, feelings and thoughts as ordinary people living through a focussed period of mis-trust between brothers and sisters from the same Church is staggering to contemplate. No doubt that the perfected saints will live under and in the spiritual provision of heaven, much as Noah and his family endured in the vessel for fourty days. And then finally great rejoicing from within the ranks of the saints as the bowls finally start toppling the strength of this dominant kingdom and false Christ towards the end of these one thousand two hundred and sixty days. We contemplated that the end of these evil days will in all likelihood be in March or April during the feast of unleavened bread. And we should sense that from the fall of this dominance period to the sudden appearance of Jesus Christ on the feast of tabernacles or trumpets during September or October of the same year there is a bit of a respite or earie quietness and expectation on the earth. We can sense this if we consider Jesus' description of this period in Matthew 24: 29 to 31 where He describes that immediately after these events the sun will be darkened and the moon will not give its light and the stars will fall from the heavens with the shaking of powers of the heavens. Followed by the star sign of the imminent return of Jesus Christ on the clouds with power and great glory. With the sounding of the trumpet His angels will gather His elect from the four corners of the Earth, to meet Him in the skies.

I have met many Christians who use the excuse that only God knows when these events will ensue. You could make out an argument using a singular verse such as Mark 13: 32 (NIV) that this could be correct: "But about that day or hour no one knows, not even the angels in heaven, nor the Son, but only the Father." Gleaning context from this singular verse, however, presents a grave misinterpretation. To misinterpret this verse in isolation and believe that the people of God should not interpret the times in which they live, is, in a sense, like imitating an ostrich who sticks his head in the ground when he sees danger approaching. Again, if you read and misinterpret this verse you will overlook that Jesus actually intimates that, as a Christian, you must always be prepared, because the signs of the end might come in your generation! In the same verses pre- and post of Mark 13: 32, Jesus informs us that God will never catch His prepared people off-guard and that His people will know and can interpret mysteries that even the angels in heaven would wish to be privy. An abundance of verses warn Christians to be on guard and interpret the times in which they reside. In Mark 13 there prove to be many:

1. "You must be on your guard." Verse 13
2. "When you see 'the abomination that causes

desolation.'" Verse 14

3. "So be on your guard; I have told you everything ahead of time." Verse 23
4. "Now learn this lesson from the fig tree: As soon as its twigs get tender and its leaves come out, you know that summer is near. Even so, when you see these things happening, you know that it is near, right at the door." Verse 28
5. "Be on guard! Be alert! You do not know when that time will come." Verse 33

Wow. Only in these scant verses do we get an impression of Jesus or a parent showing concern for the dangerous period to come. Only in these scant verses do we see a warning to His children to be awake and keep lookout; to interpret the signs; to interpret their surroundings in time – lest they be caught off guard (not so much for the coming of Jesus Christ but for the anti-Christ!).

16 FALSE PROPHETS (DEPENDENCY)

Even in the early days of the Apostles and in the days of Paul they wrote about the anti-Christ or rather the spirit of the anti-Christ. The Apostle John mentioned in his writings that even in his days, some two thousand years ago, there were already activity of the anti-Christ. It would therefore benefit us if we can see the working of or identify the works of the anti-Christ. If we can identify the spirit in which the anti-Christ operates, we will and can guard ourselves from being deceived into such a ministry in our Churches.

In order to do that we must first look at the Spirit in which Jesus Christ operated and still operates today. When we read Old Testament we could identify Jesus Christ as the veil separating the entrance to the Most Holy area of the Tabernacle as referred to in Exodus 36: 35. Prior to Christ, who was equal to God, taking the lowest position in heaven, and then coming to earth, taking the bottommost place amongst men by sacrificing Himself, He was the separation between us and God the Father. In order for us to come to the Father, He had to sacrifice Himself and be torn from top to bottom, in order for us to come through Him into the presence of the Father. Therefore in order for us to come to the Father, and have relationship with the Father as sons and daughters, we have to come through Jesus Christ and in the power of the Holy Spirit. There is simply no other way. And we see that even in Jesus Christ's own ministry, He always facilitated people to come through Him into direct relationship with the Father. We can refer to the New Testament texts where the rich young man came to Jesus for ministry. When the young man calls Jesus "good Lord", Jesus immediately moves out of the way and allow the young man to come through Him into direct relationship with God the Father with Jesus Himself saying to the young man: "why do you call Me good Lord, there is only one that is good, and that is God the Father". Jesus laid down His life in order for Himself to facilitate us coming through Him into direct relationship with the Father. Therefore Isaiah prophesied of a day where each one of us will be in direct relationship with the Father, through Jesus Christ, in the power of the Holy Spirit, and with no one teaching us any longer. Therefore the Spirit of true ministry in Christ is always, with the emphasis on always, to facilitate through our discipleship that the individual or congregation moves past us, and directly through Christ into direct relationship with the Father in the power of the Spirit. Therefore we facilitate only and in the process of discipling make the person being discipled non-dependant on us, and dependant on God the Father in direct relationship, whether it is for relationship, for light, for mercy, for teaching, for word, for healing for prophecy and for everything good that God the Father is the source of. Through facilitating a direct relationship with the Father the individual, disciple or congregant must be weaned off of the reliance on us as leaders and into reliance on God the Father, in the process surpassing and making us sort of redundant in that relationship. That is what Jesus Christ came for, sacrificed and offered Himself for and ultimately died and was resurrected for – that each individual have access to abundant life through Him with God the Father. This everlasting life commences for this disciple if he or she can see, hear and know God the Father for themselves. The persons only matures to perfection if they themselves start every morning living a daily sacrificial life with their body and senses in personal holiness and purity in communion with the Father. Commence their sacrificial day toward the Father with their tongue and lips in in thanksgiving towards God and honouring brothers and sister and all men in the day. And then importantly balancing that with themselves moving into a position to bring offerings of their time, talents and not only their treasure ministering diligently in their Christian community. That is the Spirit of Jesus Christ.

The anti-Christ or anti-spirit is a spirit of reliance or slavery to an individual leader, a prophet, an institution or ultimately to a false-Christ. Many, many, many preachers, pastors, prophets, healers and teachers since the days Jesus ascended to heaven naturally tend to make individuals, disciples, congregants and entire congregations dependant on them. They never seem to get it right to facilitate the individual's progress beyond them, and through Christ Jesus in the power of the Holy Spirit to grow into spiritual maturity into good ministry works in relationship directly with God their Father. Week after week, and year after year individuals and entire congregations are kept reliant on the input and talents of their leaders or teachers or prophets. The spirit of the anti-Christ is to nurture reliance on an individual that gives them their frequently needed dose of the word, or healing, or counselling, or prophetic word. That as opposed to showing, facilitating and maturing the saint to get it for themselves through their daily relationship with God the Father. This anti-Christ spirit aims to keep the individual or congregation dependant on the facilitator's input, week after week. Subsequently making the individual reliant on the input of their leader, as opposed to being assisted to grow towards maturity to enter in themselves and growing to the point of leading and diligently serving others in the congregation. The anti-Christ spirit is therefore partially on any man that continually seeks the limelight and retains the ministry position – as opposed to making the individual or congregation grow themselves into mature sons and daughters of God, in order to in turn themselves serve other disciples to later achieve the same.

The essence of the book of Revelation therefore reverts back to this issue of dependence. Imagine for a second that the whole book of Revelation is painting the picture of two woman. The one woman is pure and the other a harlot. Both woman start of the same way... they each represent the sanctuary of God... and as shown in Ezekiel 24: 21 it facilitate that God the Father is the boast, desire and the delight of each person's soul that enters. In other words, each of the woman represents the Church. The pure woman is distinguished by straddling increasingly the Kingdom of God and led by the Holy Spirit to mature sons and daughters increasingly into perfected saints. These sons and daughters build the new Jerusalem through their ministry and works which is ultimately given to Jesus Christ as a wedding gift.

On the inverse the other woman also starting off representing the sanctuary of God increasingly straddles the kingdom of men, the beast, led by the material obsession for riches of relationships, finances and health. In this spirit her sons and daughters are kept dependant on their religious leaders as representatives of God and not grown to maturity to themselves minister to their communities. Their way and works also build a city – Babylon – which is ultimately given a wedding gift to the anti-Christ!!! A sobering picture that had John, who wrote Revelation, stagger to a standstill when he was shown the Harlot – how God's sanctuary could evolve to represent a prostitute. What we have to realize here is that just as the book of Jeremia or Ezekiel but so also the book of Revelation would never talk about a prostitute or a harlot... unless she started of as a woman of God, pure and representing His sanctuary. But then through adhering and pursuing rather the idols of men, as opposed to the Spirit of God, she is slowly transformed into a harlot – with her offspring of sons and daughters doomed for destruction. It is a sobering picture that draw you to a standstill - just as John experienced when shown the vision in Revelation.

17 REVELATION – PER CHAPTER

"Woe to you who desire the day of the Lord!... Is not the day of the Lord darkness, and not light? " Amos 5: 18 & 20

T he purpose of this Chapter is to run a quick overview of the chapters as we encounter them in Revelation. We will not address every verse, or try and re-write or explain the entire book here for ourselves. Rather, the purpose would rather be to take the keys that we developed in earlier chapters and see if it unlocks a story line for us and guide us soberly and meditatively through the entire Book. Hopefully, if all goes well we could try and summarize it all on one or two pages or diagram/s. If we can summarize of simplify it for ourselves into such a summary – we should be able to in turn teach others on the same subject. What we will do is move linearly through entire chapters in order to keep it practical. What we should do is take our Bible and read the entire Chapter/s for ourselves as we move through each section, to make our experience much deeper and richer. In so doing not adding or deleting anything that the Bible teaches itself. Let's go!

Chapter 1: in New Testament verses we see that Jesus Christ loves us and calls us His friends. And He continues to say that as our friend He shows or tells us everything. If we love Him and we call Him our friend then we are obliged to obey His command. Through His love and friendship we are told everything. As we meditate on Jesus' words it will quickly light up in us that His command stems from friendship and from love – and therefore the command is always life-giving to us. In this chapter we are greeted with grace and peace by God the Father sitting on the throne, by the Holy Spirit (seven Spirits) standing before the throne, and by Jesus Christ our brother as the first born from the dead and ruler over the kings of the earth. We should stop here for a minute and meditate that it is God the Father that is on the throne, and that the Father is called the "who is and who was and who is to come" – or Yahweh as He introduced Himself to Moses also. And further that the Holy Spirit stands in front of the Father's throne. And that even Jesus Christ calls Him God and Father. Jesus is seen here as the first born from the dead, the first fruit. And that we are washed in Jesus' blood making us the next to be born from the dead, or kings & priests, or second fruits if you will, or brothers and sisters of Jesus before God our Father. John then introduces himself in this Chapter, and is then taken in the Spirit to the Temple in heaven, where Jesus Christ is dressed as the high priest doing duty in the Temple. Jesus identifies Himself as the Alpa (first letter of the Greek alphabet) and Omega (the last letter of the alphabet), and significantly uses more or less a similar description of His name to that of the Father namely: "I am He who lives, and was dead, and behold, I am alive forever more".

Chapter 2 and 3: in these two Revelation chapters we see messages to seven churches spanning from 34 AD to now – the Church era. In order for us to measure the messages to each one of these churches we refer back to our discussion on how a church should minister to disciples by growing each one of them to a perfected saint. To refresh our memories we insert that diagram here as we read for ourselves through the message to each one of the Churches. Their discipleship is being measured by a reed that more or less parallels our diagram:

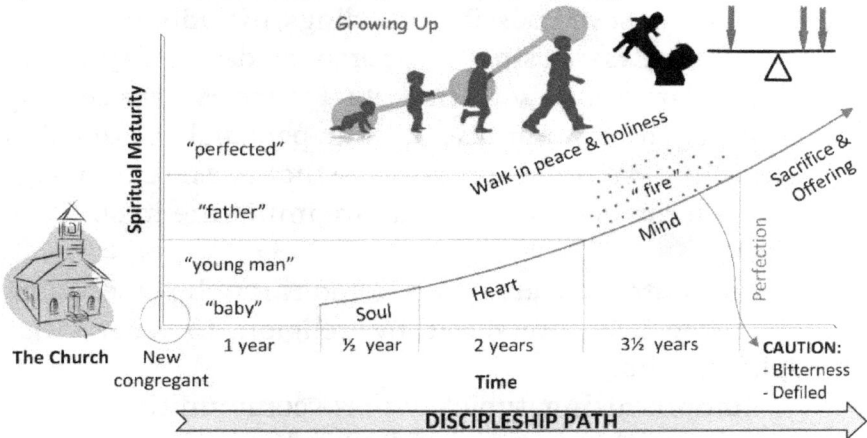

In this diagram we see a person entering the community of a Church, and after hearing the Gospel preached is effectively taken on a discipleship path where they are Spiritually conceived as babies through repentance, believing in Jesus Christ, baptised in water, and hands laid on them to receive the Holy Spirit. They are taught how to spend quality morning by morning time with God the Father nurturing their first love to grow into young men in the Spirit. When fire touches their relationships, or finances or health they are assisted and shown how to stand in rest, quietness and confidence through this growth phase by fiery trial to become fathers in the Spirit. Now walking a daily life of sacrifice keeping their bodies in holiness and purity, and their tongue to honour God and men. This is the one side of the balancing act. That is balanced by walking a life of serving diligently in their Christian community. In this equilibrium their faith grows – and they walk as perfected Saints. In this way by growing perfected Saints the Church achieves the vision given by Paul in Ephesians that the body will edify itself in love. Now with this picture in mind, we read Jesus' seven messages to the Churches in Revelation chapters 2 and 3.

We could reason these messages were for those seven historic churches. However, we could also rather categorise the status of our own faith, or that of our congregation, or measure any Church in terms of seven possible standings, including:

- **Loveless**: losing our personal day-to-day secret place relationship with God our Father. We are serving diligently in community, but our personal relationship is waning. We could contemplate that our hearts engage easily in material matters but are immature in Spiritual affairs.

- **Persecuted**: we are being tested through persecution, and especially pressured by religion to forego our Spiritual living.

- **Compromising**: typically these communities are city bound and the pressure of fleshly living detracts from living in the Spirit. These idols include focus on sexual things, food, clothes, high living standards for housing and cars etc. If we assume Paul's words meant living 90% as a father in the things of the Spirit and living 10% as an infant in the things of the flesh... the compromising saints have this upside down. In the extreme instances we would find ourselves engaging warmly and easily with our heart's feelings and soul's emotions toward the fleshly riches. Engagement towards such unknowingly impact our praise and worship and a discerned eye and ear will measure it as dull. The compromise however often come that our mind does not reason to keep to the commands of Christ to walk in purity and holiness, often with large immoral compromises to be found under the surface of the community.

- **Corrupt**: we forego the authority given in our community and homes that it is first God, then Jesus, then the husband and then the wife. The Jezebel spirit is a female spirit of rebellion that overtake the Church, where women rebel against the God given authority for men to take Spiritual leadership, and where men renege on their Spiritual responsibility to serve diligently with their time, talents and treasure. A picture given by God the Father is one whereby as you move downwards from God the Father to Jesus Christ to the husband to the wife this downward communion style is that of love. However on the return leg from women to men to Christ to the Father the communication style should be that of respect. If we get that wrong we are in rebellion e.g. if men love Christ but expect Christ to respect us it just instinctively sounds wrong doesn't it?

- **Dead**: these are religious based people. They go to Church, but there is no Spiritual discipleship growth path toward what God would term growth toward perfection (or Christlikeness if you will). And therefore Jesus comments: "I have not found your works perfect before God". On closer analysis we would find that in worship we limit God to our mind's thoughts, ideas and understanding. We do not engage with our body's strength, heart's feelings and with our soul's emotions. We limit God to what we think and can understand with our reasoning only, which become quite evident and visible when we observe the stiffness of our own praise and worship.

- **Faithfull**: we could all stop at this message meant for us and for our Church community and dwell on it a little. The key message to note here is the command to persevere. Note to ourselves these people, or community or church is kept from the hour of trial coming over the whole world. Does that mean rapture? Or does that mean like Noah in his boat when the storm hits, we have to ask ourselves – like in the days of Noah?

- **Lukewarm**: this individual, community or church has not experienced the "fire" or testing phase of normal Christian growth to reach the growth phase of a father. Therefore real deep Spiritual character is lacking that only comes from a deep baptism in fire through trials and tribulation.

Chapter 4, 5 and 6: We are back in 34 AD right after the ascension of Jesus Christ from the earth into the third heaven where this scene plays out. God is seen sitting on the throne with a scroll sealed with seven seals in His right hand. And only Jesus, that was slain, is found worthy to take this scroll from God's hand, loose the seals and look into and read the scroll. In it is the names of those redeemed to God the Father out of every tribe, tongue, people and nation to follow in Jesus' footsteps to become kings and priests (or children) to God our Father. Here in 34 AD there is a great contrast between the Kingdom of God and the kingdom of men, with the kingdom of men flourishing in hate, pride and rapidly becoming all powerful with its own interpretation of religion, economic system, financial system, and military prowess. All in contrast to the proven systems that work in the Kingdom of God. And in 34 AD with the breaking of the seven seals evil forces are allowed to be released to hamper the otherwise unchecked growth of man's kingdom (or the beast from the sea). Initially small in their immediate impact in 34 AD, these forces unlocked by the breaking of each seal would grow increasingly stronger and in the process sow exponentially more havoc in the earth. The first seal unleashes a white conquering spirit of nation against nation... but also gains for the enemy in the area of the Church (the tars being sown in the field of the Church). The second seal unleashes conflict and takes peace from the earth, leading to people killing and war against each other. The third seal broken unleashes disturbances in the economic and financial systems of measure created by men, and leads to scarcity. Especially in the area of monetary remuneration a man receives less and less in the face of his daily sweat. The forth seal calls out systematic and increasing incidences of death to kill with violence, hunger, plague, and through animals. With the breaking of the fifth seal the martyrs from the Old Testament e.g. Isaiah was sawn in half, is seen temporarily waking from their sleep and asking that God take vengeance on their spilt blood. They are given robes and asked to go back to sleep a little longer – meaning the time of the Church era is short (in God's terms a little over two days only). When the sixth seal is broken, there are great cosmic disturbances and a sign in the sky. From the sun, to the moon to falling stars. Including great and increasingly larger earthquakes. We can track these events of the chapter in our growing picture below:

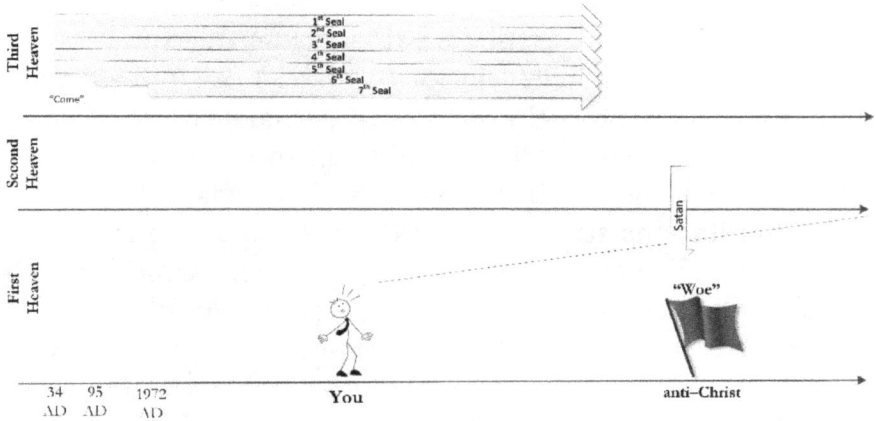

Chapter 7: In this Chapter of Revelation we encounter four angels that we will again encounter in Revelation 9 verse 14. They are instructed to hold back for a little while until Revelation 9. They are instructed to refrain from unleashing four destructive winds on the earth until 144 000 servants of God are marked on their foreheads. We can only guess that this seal on their foreheads is in contrast to the 6-6-6 seal that we will encounter later in Revelation. This seal in chapter seven is probably the seal 7-7-7. With the mentioning of this here in chapter 7 we cannot imagine that this is a chip, or an implant or a tattoo or anything physical. Rather it is a Spiritual marking, which if we had to use our intuition would represent soul redemption (Holy Spirit), heart redemption (God the Father) and mind redemption (Jesus Christ) of these Saints, giving them a Spiritual marking on their foreheads and right hand... visible in the spiritual as the number 7-7-7. We also contemplated in an

earlier sketch that the first seven represents the Kingdom of God where the Father is on the throne. The pure woman or the Church led by the Holy Spirit representing the second number. And the final number seven representing the new Jerusalem represented by the works of the sons and daughters born and matured through the pure woman and which city is given to Jesus Christ as worthy gift. A number of things that we can note for ourselves in Revelation 7: 1 to 8 is that these 144 000 saints are all male servants. That they are already identified and chosen before the four angels in Revelation 9: 13 to 21 can unleash their destruction. And that these 144 000 male servants most probably aligns with the "male child" taken up into heaven in Revelation 12: 2 and specifically verse 5 of that chapter. And that this male child consisting of 144 000 has the unique quality that they would rule the nations with a rod of iron, which sounds similar to the type of rule that Jesus Christ would rule with when He returns. We could therefore put all these puzzle pieces together for ourselves when we read here of the 144 000 male servants. These are men that is chosen and discipled through a process of soul, heart and mind redemption and learn to walk as perfected saints. Our best guess would be that these men are not concentrated in one area of the globe or from one specific Church... but rather through discipleship and circumstances guided by the hand of God to grow them to perfection. We can on the balance of probabilities say that the woman giving birth represents the entire picture or ripeness of the woman, from the time of Abraham to our current Churches as we know them. These men are born and discipled in the Spirit because the time of the woman has matured to this point and is now ready to Spiritually birth and mature these Saints. At the same time the beast from the sea, remember that this represents the matured kingdom of man, has matured to tear this "male child" to pieces – on balance of probability not wanting to allow this "male child" to rule over this kingdom with an iron sceptre. We can then only imagine for ourselves that as these men come to spiritual perfection, they will become a threat to the beast from the sea.

And because the time for the rule of Christ only comes after the rule of the anti-Christ, these 144 000 men will be taken up, or raptured if you like, into heaven to return only later with Jesus to rule. The 144 000 taken up an away return only after at least three-and-a-half years. We can only imagine for ourselves that in heaven they will prepare to return with Jesus Christ for His millennium rule with a sceptre of iron. We can imagine their preparation with Jesus in heaven in Revelation chapter 14: 1. Are these men only from the tribe of Israel we might ask ourselves? And the answer is probably not, but rather from the entire body of Christ, because in Jesus Christ we are all made one with Israel and the promises given to Abraham.

In Revelation 7: 9 to 17 we see the rest of the Christians, other than the 144 000. This passage encompass numerous clues that we should take note of, if we are not one of the 144 000 chosen and taken up into heaven during the process of manifestation of the anti-Christ. The first clue is in verse 9 that states "after these things". And "these things" relate to at least the 144 000 men taken up into heaven and at least the unleashing of the four winds of destruction described in Revelation 9: 13 to 21. But then more specifically in verse 14 of Revelation 7 we see that all the remainder Saints now seen in heaven are described as: "These are the ones who come out of the great tribulation and washed their robes and made them white in the blood of the Lamb". If we fast forward again to the sign in the stars in Revelation 12 and specifically verse 17 we see the Dragon (Satan) thrown out of heaven going out to "make war with the rest of her (that is the pure woman) offspring, who keep the commandments of God and have the testimony of Jesus Christ". We therefore see that apart from the 144 000 men taken up early into heaven to prepare them for Christ's return, the other Christians (termed here as other offspring) have to stand and walk through the three-and-a-half year tribulation period of the anti-Christ. And only with the second coming of Jesus Christ thereafter are we taken up to heaven to meet with Jesus. The 144 000 that return with Jesus remain on the earth, jointly with the Saints decapitated during the rule of the anti-Christ. These rule on earth for the seventh day or millennial rule of Christ.

Chapter 8: At the opening of this chapter we are taken back into heaven, for the breaking of the seventh seal by Jesus. Following this we encounter a half an hour silence (probably equating to nearly 21 years here on the earth). We can only imagine that the silence in heaven is to contemplate and empathise with us as people on earth for the impact of the events to come. Once the silence is broken we encounter four angels blasting their trumpets in quick succession. With the sounding of the first we see that a third of the earths trees and grass is burned up. Again it is events that start small and exponentially increases in severity as time passes. From the time it starts it increases year on year. With the second trumpet a third of the sea becomes uninhabitable for all kinds of sea creatures, and in the process destroying the livelihoods of people who used to make their living from the sea. The third blast affects what we would call potable water fit for human consumption. A thirds of these sources either dry up, become polluted or turn toxic for us to utilise to stimulate economic growth. The fourth trumpet affects the sun, moon and stars with increasing cosmic activity in signs to the sun, the moon and meteor showers. From where we are standing today as we read these prophecies we can intrinsically relate much better with these events than say somebody reading it when the book of Thessalonica was written nearly 2000 years ago, don't you think? What should be of greater concern to us today is the loud voice declaring the successive woe-woe-woe accompanying trumpet five, six and seven. Trumpet five is a five month plague. Trumpet six a third of mankind is killed. And trumpet seven commences the rule of the anti-Christ. We can summarise chapter 8 in the accompanying picture:

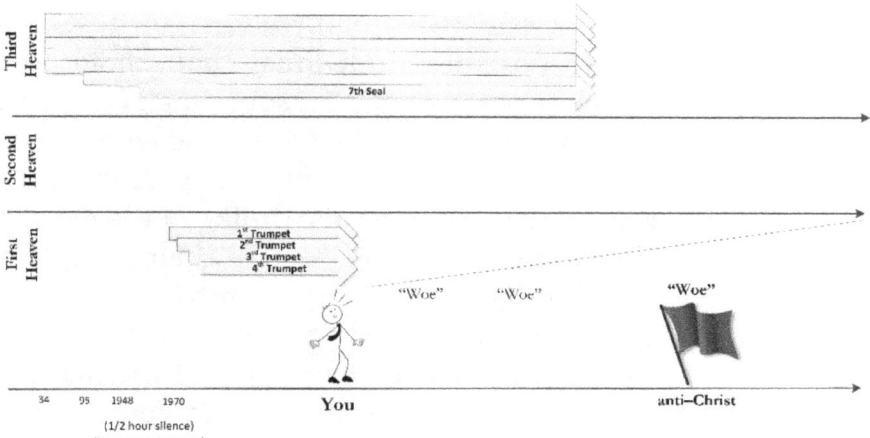

Chapter 9: From chapter 9 onwards we see a sudden preparation of the Church, the pure woman, through what we can term three mercy events, two of which appear in Revelation 9. We observe that the state of readiness of the Churches are measured during these events that suddenly overcome the Churches. We all know that each individual Christian and especially each Church believes that their discipleship path is a "holy cow"? Well, during the ensuing events of Revelation chapters 9, 10 and 11 we will stand surprised how our own and our respective current corporate theologies and programs will fall short of giving us the state of preparedness answers that we actually require. Both the duration of and the impact of the events will pull our theologies apart during this seven year period, and show that our discipleship programs fall short of God's expectations. God wants perfected saints, and we will be shown up in our efforts of our existing programs. There will be only two responses from individuals and respective Churches during this seven year period. The one half will repent and take testimony from perfected saints to lead their people toward discipleship paths for the preparation of perfected saints. The other half will become embittered and fall away from the way that God always intended, exposing themselves to the deception that God Himself will send with the advent of the anti-Christ. In

Revelation 9: 1 to 12 the first mercy event to test the preparedness of each Christian individual, household and community overcomes our world with the sounding of the fifth trumpet. A plague ensues that only touches people who do not have the 7-7-7 seal (sign of a mature, or perfected, or Christlikeness) of God on their foreheads. Unlike in the days of Covid where people begged physicians to save their lives, this contrary will see people begging their caretakers to rather assist them to die. But death will evade us for five months. What you have to see here is that through the testimony of the marked Saints, many, rather multitudes will repent and come under effective discipleship and be healed. We could refer to it as a sort of revival period if you will. Perhaps the words of the old-testament prophet is more accurate that the perfected Saints will witness wonderful and victorious crusades during this period. In the Spirit this plague will be visible, and have a specific sound – we will have to wait and see whether it will be so in the flesh also, but perhaps not. What we do however know is that it will be directly from the darkest depths of the earth, evil, and unlike anything we had time to prepare for. It will definitely show up the weaknesses in our armour, with the intended purpose for us to fix where we fall short.

Scarcely have we dealt with this event, and suddenly we are overtaken by the next trumpet blast. All that we know is that this is a major event in quick succession to the previous plague. And here we encounter fire, smoke and brimstone killing a third of the world population. That is in anyone's book a major catastrophe, that suddenly overtakes us and tests us to our limits of preparedness toward perfected saints. We could muse, as many do, that this is caused by a nuclear war between two super powers, assuming a third world war lead by the United States of America against China and her allies respectively. However, the beast from the Sea (representing the dominant human kingdom) is unlikely to tear itself to pieces right toward the end, and at best the USA could represent the body of the beast itself and China one of ten horns on the beast.

But them attacking each other would be similar to a dragon starting to eat itself by its tail – and that just instinctively feels wrong, doesn't it? We could therefore also start thinking in the direction of major global volcanic activity over an extended period of three years. Imagining a world population of nine billion people, losing a third of the population is a catastrophic event over a three year span! Again, what the perfected saints will encounter during this period is major victory discipling saints toward perfection for the Kingdom of God through effective teaching and testimony. It is a revival in the Christian community, where the testimony of these mature saints will see half of the Christian population following in their discipleship footsteps toward preparedness. Sadly and surprisingly however we also see that a great number of people and especially known Christians, whether individuals or corporate, do not repent and adopt a path towards growing toward that of perfected Saints. If we meditate on this it is quite difficult to fathom and sad indeed, especially at this late stage of what is yet to come.

Chapter 10 and 11: In chapter 10 we note that this mighty angel announces that with the sounding of the seventh trumpet there will be no more delay and the mystery that God intended would be finished, or made known. With John eating the message brought by the angel, it initially is sweet in his mouth, but churns his stomach. In other words, it initially sounds promising that Jesus is returning, but the coming of the deceiver prior to that, and especially the wilful falling away of at least half of the current church is a stomach churner for John. We can also make a note here for ourselves that if we wish to grow our feeling or understanding for these spiritual pictures sketched in Revelation we could also turn to the Old Testament prophets to grow our observation. Specifically for this instance of the eating of this scroll we could turn to Ezekiel having to do the same when God shows him the picture of the kingdom (Isreal or Judah), the sanctuary or the woman (Samaria and Jerusalem's sanctuary) turned harlot and the destruction of the cities Samaria and Jerusalem with their respective off-spring of sons and daughters... see Ezekiel 3: 2 to 3. What we can deduct from both Revelation and Ezekiel is that this bitter word in the stomach is not for foreign people, but for God's people, for people in His sanctuary of the Church. And we learn that only His representative sanctuary on earth or woman or church can be called either faithful and pure or conversely disobedient to His ways and subsequently a harlot woman. It is not a word for strangers, but for a woman that is meant to live in intimacy with Him only. For this word to sink in perhaps read Ezekiel 3: 1 to 15 contemplatively again. And then realise that the scroll word here in Revelation, sweet as honey in the mouth because it is words from a Lover to His own people, turns bitter in the stomach because they are found to have turned away from His ways.

We then witness the appearance of the final two witnesses. This is the last mercy event for individual Christians and Churches to repent and follow the same message that was witnessed by perfected saints during the events of the fifth and sixth trumpets. We see many similarities to what transpired in the days of the prophet Elijah in the old testament, when we consider the three-and-a-half year drought Elijah proclaimed. And to get a feeling for who or what this Elijah would be like, we have to imagine John the Baptist as also being referred to as Elijah. In other words one of the persons will act in the spirit of Elijah... because John the Baptist was not physically Elijah. We can expect one person acting in a spirit of "fire" or leadership or spirit of Moses. And the other person acting in a spirit of "water" or baptism or spirit of Elijah. This is a time of measurement. We would want to imagine for ourselves that Christians and the Church will receive the words of the last two Witnesses with open hands and hearts. But alas their words to be discipled in the way of reaching the growth stage of perfected saints will be most unpopular to a vast majority of Christians. Still with a very unpopular message towards the end of a three-and-a-half year period, the anti-Christ will ascend and have these two final witnesses killed. Indeed, there will be a great rejoicing within a large part of the Christian community that was plagued by these two witnesses to adhere to their message. And with their ascension into heaven the second of the three woes are past, with the third woe representing the coming of the deceit represented during a three and a half year rule of Satan, the anti-Christ and the kingdom represented by the beast from the sea of people. And with this the seventh trumpet sounds!

Chapter 12: this chapter in Revelation represents a sign in the stars that summarises the flow of events that we have already considered. Here we see the pure woman that we discussed in earlier chapters, being confronted with the beast from the sea that we considered in detail. The beast threatening to tear a specific child of hers, consisting of 144 000 men, to pieces. In other words the chapter says that a sign in the heavens and ripeness of times will herald in these events. We do not require a degree in theology to see that the woman represents all the Biblical events that took place since the promises given to Abraham that his descendants born will eventually be called children of God. And as the woman matures from the time God gives Abraham the promise, approximately 2025 years after we met Adam in the garden of Eden or 1735 year before the birth of Jesus, we now meet her here in Revelation 12 pregnant with a special male child. This child is destined to rule the Nations with an iron rod, and instinctively we know that this male child refers to the 144 000 men described in Revelation 7: 1 to 8 and Revelation 14: 1 to 5. The dragon that appears at the time of the birth of this male child is described as the dragon from the sea with its body, its seven heads and the ten horns – and represents the unified kingdom of the world. These Nations that would not want to see these 144 000 men rule over them. Interesting enough we see that this beast from the sea, manages to drag one third of the angels or the fallen angels to the earth. With the threat to extinguish these men, the 144 000 men are taken up into heaven. The woman (the pure woman of a Spirit filled church) that give birth to Christians is now seen to flee into the wilderness for the period of the tribulation or for the three-and-a-half year rule of the anti-Christ. Satan himself is also thrown to the earth to deceive and allowed to roam the earth for this tumultuous period. The final of three woes heralds in this period where Satan, the beast from the sea representing a unified world kingdom, and a deceiving-Christ has free reign in the world and especially in the church to deceive. The dragon, not being able to kill the male child, persecutes and pursues the woman. Enraged that the woman cannot be reached during this period, Satan makes war with all the other Christians that was birthed by the woman.

Chapter 13: is descriptive of the beast from the sea, that we now know represents the unification of Nations or rather governments that will rule during the tribulation period. We mused that the body of the beast could in all likelihood be represented by a super power nation similar to a United States of America, which was formed by the seven kingdoms that gave rise to their style of governance (including Babylon, Medes & Persia, Greece, Roman Empire, mixed Roman Empire, mid-evil Europe, and modern Europe). With the upcoming ten kingdoms that will grow dominant on the back of the body of the beast, including perhaps the likes of Russia, Turkey, Iran, Ethiopia, Libia, Brazil, India, China, South Africa and probably Egypt. Great authority, power and the throne to rule is given to this beast by Satan. The beast will speak through a unified mouth... and will during this 42 month period blaspheme (mis-represent God the Father, Jesus Christ and the Holy Spirit) against everything pertaining to the kingdom of God. We have to be careful if we use the word blaspheme here... because it is a period of deception. In other words the sanctuary of God is during these times represented by a Church that in actual fact is later shown to resemble the prostitute or a harlot, or a number six, which is a human endeavour closely resembling but not accurately representing the Holy Spirit (representing a number seven). This beast will also make war against the saints, and will sadly overcome them. Everyone will succumb to worshipping this beast, except the saints who is written in the Book of Life of the slain Lamb. The saints are called upon to show patience and faith during this period, based on the knowledge that those who capture and kill them during this period will be captured and killed during the vengeance of the soon to come Jesus Christ.

The height of the deceit during this 42 month period will be the appearance of a person in the likeness of Christ to deceive the Church. He will be granted authority, and perform great signs in order to deceive. It is possible that the imagery during the rule of the Roman Empire, that was visible during Jesus Christ's time, will re-emerge in order for people to worship these images. The mark on the forehead and right hand, probably a spiritual rather than a physical marking, will be 6-6-6 or a deceitful mimic of the discipling of how a Christian receives 7-7-7 on their forehead and right hand. We can therefore imagine for ourselves that during this three-and-a-half year period disciples of the anti-Christ will repent, believe, be baptised, and receive a false spirit of the beast and discipled to grow in soul, heart and mind to mature under discipleship during this period.

Chapter 14: in Revelation chapter 14 we meet the 144 000 men that represent the male child that will be taken up into heaven. We meet them here as perfected saints in heaven and can see that the name of the Father is written on their foreheads namely 7-7-7. There are numerous characteristics given to these men including singing a new song as if from many waters (every nation, tribe, tongue and people) before the throne and they are inseparable from Christ and wherever He goes they follow. They were redeemed (soul, heart and mind i.e. perfected saints) from the earth and represent the first of many to follow their example. With this we see the proclamation of the ensuing judgement to come over the kingdom of the anti-Christ and proclamation of the toppling of the city that represents the height of this human kingdom. A special blessing is spoken over all the Christians who will die in the Lord during the rule of the anti-Christ. The completion of the picture of Jesus' parable of the wheat and tars are given here... on how the tars that was planted amongst God's people is first harvested during the fall of the kingdom of the anti-Christ. To complete the picture of the tars or grapes pressed in the wine press Revelation 14: 14 to 20 must be read with Isaiah's complete description in Isaiah 5: 1 to 7. Here we see that God's judgement begins with His own field, in our case the Church, that yields "wild grapes" or "tars" if you will as opposed the kingly grapes which is only harvested afterward. Both crushed in the winepress... but each yielding different end results or products, they taste and smell completely different is the likeness image that should settle in our minds.

Chapter 15 & 16: we observe the global events that ensue when God pours out bowl after bowl of His wrath on the kingdom of Satan, the height of man's kingdom and their leader the anti-Christ. We see that the Temple in heaven is filled with smoke from the glory of God and from His power. And no one can enter in during the outpouring of the seven bowls and until their ensuing plagues are completed. We can again note that many of these spiritual sketches, such as the Glory of God filling the Temple, are repetitive of images shown in books such as Jeremia and Ezekiel when God poured His wrath over either Israel and Judah.

Even during the ensuing events, we notice that man's heart is non-repentant and does not give glory to God. We have to insert here again that if we speak of man's heart here we are talking of what we would term Christians today! During these events the kings of the Nations draw up for battle against Israel. From the description of noises and thundering and lightnings we can derive that war ensues. God wins this war with the plague of exceedingly great hailstones.

Chapter 17: in this section the scarlet woman is shown in comparison to the image of the pure woman of Revelation 12: 1. The words describing this scarlet woman is similar to Old Testament images of a woman that was unfaithful to her Husband – God the Father. Words such as great harlot, committed fornication and drunk with the wine of her fornication convey a message of a woman unfaithful to her Husband. Similarly as we described the imagery of a pure woman, the church led by the Holy Spirit, riding on the Spirit Kingdom of God the Father... here this scarlet woman is depicted as riding on a scarlet beast depicting the kingdom of men. It all speaks of a church-era gone wrong choosing the fleshly tangible creations of men as opposed to the intangible that requires greater discernment to see the reality of the Spirit. This picture of this scarlet woman, familiar to us as a part of the Church today, is depicted here adorned in purple and scarlet with gold and precious stones and pearls. It is so hard to imagine that this woman could remotely be representative of a large part of the Church today... so much so that even John said: "I marvelled with great amazement". John last saw and knew the Church in its birth stages... and now seeing her here as the scarlet woman was beyond comprehension. We should note Revelation 17: 14 that the Lamb, Jesus Christ, overcame this worldly rule of nations and the accompanying religion of the scarlet woman, and with Him all those that are called His chosen and His faithful stand outside or above this system.

Interestingly we see that the unpure woman is established amongst all nations, tribes, languages and kingdoms. Grippingly enough we see that the ten final kingdoms that rule in unity of one mind during and give their power to the beast during the three-and-a-half year period of the anti-Christ rule is themselves the cause for the ultimate implosion of the anti-Christ empire or period of rule. It is they themselves that turn on the harlot woman sitting on the beast, see Revelation 17: 16, toward the height of the one thousand two hundred and sixty day period. And the whole house, rule, and unity of the anti-Christ come tumbling down from within as a house divided and in rebellion against itself cannot stand.

Chapter 18: if we recall our salt and pepper analogy and discussion the picture that is sketched is that first of a kingdom, followed by the sanctuary or woman, that then gives birth to sons and daughters. These then through the way that they choose to walk and their works or actions causes a city to rise. As the book of Revelation contrasts two sanctuaries or women, one pure and the other a harlot, with one husband God the Father the choices of each of the woman result in two separate cities being born, the one the new Jerusalem and the other termed Babylon. And here in Revelation 18 we are given a glimpse of the physical manifestation of a woman that chooses the riches of man (relationships, finances and health) over the Spiritual choices of the Spirit of the Lord, the Spirit of knowledge, the Spirit of wisdom, the Spirit of understanding, the Spirit of council, the Spirit of might and the Spirit of the fear of God. The children born out of this communion between the unified kingdom of men, and man's interpretation of the sanctuary of the Church, has the result of men and woman that mature in soul, heart and mind and that build a system, a culture, an economy, politics, a financial framework, a legal scheme that ultimately portrays a unified city – something like a New York today. If you look at it, it is the best and highest that man can achieve… with its stock market, banking hierarchy, its culture in music and all colours, its opulence, culinary delights and so much more. It represents the highest and best man's efforts can achieve and scores a solid – 6.

And here in one hour we see this great system pulled down, destroyed never to be seen again. The kingdom, the harlotry of the sanctuary of the church with the idols of men, the men and woman born out of this communion and their resultant handiwork is destroyed. The irony is that this destruction commences as we have seen in chapter 17 with the final unified ten kingdoms turning on this illustrious woman and tearing her apart. The saints are called to come out of this city or cities and not to partake in it because of the ensuing destruction. The impact of the tearing down of this economic, financial and trade system is felt and mourned globally.

Chapter 19: we see celebrations in heaven when the great city Babylon is destroyed. And how the righteous walk and acts of the perfected saints adorn the new Jerusalem that is being prepared to be given to Jesus Christ as a gift. Those invited to the wedding feast are pointed to and called blessed – you are a guest.

From Matthew 24 we can see that following the destruction of Babylon and the judgement of the harlot woman... there is a short delay before we see Jesus Christ on His white horse with heaven's army in tow on-route to earth to rule with a rod of iron. These are wonderful passages describing Jesus Christ in all His glory and His ensuing judgement. Remember also the 144 000 that we perused earlier will be in tow to rule with Jesus with an iron sceptre over the Nations.

Kings and nations gather to war against Jesus' ensuing armies. But they are defeated. The beast and the false prophet is captured and thrown into hell. The first two things ever thrown into hell is therefore this unified governmental system of man that tried to emulate God's kingdom and the false Christ. All those deceived and whom partook in the harlot woman's sanctuary during the tribulation period is killed by Jesus's army. Note that those deceived, judged and killed are not thrown into hell, they are killed and will sleep until God's final judgement.

Chapter 20: This chapter warrants a whole study on its own. The reason being that it is a conspiracy killer. It addresses things such as the patience, endurance and long-suffering of God the Father. Whether we could expect a rapture whereby we are mysteriously taken away when Christ returns. And many more.

We note in this chapter that the serpent of old, or Satan or the devil, has taken on the form of a dragon. And mysteriously Satan himself is not thrown into hell here like the beast from the sea and the beast from the earth. No, Satan himself is bound, locked-up in the deepest pit under the earth, and sealed to prevent his deception for one thousand years.

Interesting enough we have to muse who was killed,

destroyed and removed from the chessboard up to now to determine who the real enemy was all along. Many conspiracies say it is the Muslim that will pursue the saint in the last days. Some in the past said it would be the communist. But in these chapters we noted that it was in-fact the person sitting next to us in the church pew that turned out to be the enemy. In other words if the woman representing the sanctuary practices harlotry the representation of God the Father to the surrounding neighbours, countrymen and nations go awry. And in these verses in Chapter 20 we see God the Father again setting up a new era where He is represented accurately to the Nations for their salvation.

Christ returns to earth to represent the kingdom of God the Father accurately to all the Nations that have not had the benefit of such representation. It is interesting to study here who is in Jesus Christ's entourage as He rules for a thousand years, accurately representing God the Father's kingdom – ruling with and iron sceptre. Here we see Jesus Christ Himself return. As He comes closer we can see from New Testament texts that the Christian that made it through the tribulation is taken-up into the air and in the instant of an eye given a new redeemed body. Why you might ask? Well, the answer might be to rule by His side for a 1 000 years. From these verses and from our previous consideration of the 144 000 perfected young men the following persons are said to rule with Jesus for a thousand years, including:

- The 144 000 young men as first off-spring from the pure woman in the seven years leading into the advent of the tribulation. They are taken away, seen in heaven, and then return to rule with Jesus Christ with an iron rod;
- All those who have been previously beheaded for witnessing Jesus after Jesus ascended into heaven;
- Probably those who have been previously beheaded for the word of God in the Old Testament times. We could think of examples such a Isaiah and other;

- Probably also Christians who prepared prior to and then walked through the anti-Christ tribulation period not worshipping or receiving the mark of the Beast on them. Looking at the select audience of the other persons, it gives us an idea of the severity of the tribulation period to bestow such an honour on the saint;
- It is such an honour to be placed in this select group that will rule with Jesus Christ that it is placed in a separate category on its own namely the "first resurrection". They are called blessed, and that they will not be subject to the second death – subject to the judgement day of God the Father. They are also called priest of God the Father and of Jesus Christ.

These passages unfortunately also kills some perhaps far-fetched theories. Firstly, we can assume that if a Christian passes away they go to sleep. With time not a factor any longer, with a thousand years like one day, someone like Adam has been sleeping for less than six days already. The select group that will rule with Christ for a thousand years are the only persons subject to only the first death. They will not have to stand through the judgement day of God the Father and be subject to a possible second death judgement like everyone else. Therefore Christian and non-Christian alike will therefore rise on God the Father's judgement day and will be subject to a court hearing. If found not to know the Father, who is Spirit, you will be judged harshly with a second death – namely hell. If you are found to know the Father you will be judged to receive everlasting life. The only Christians not subject to this judgement day are those serving with Jesus Christ for a thousand years.

Secondly we might ask ourselves whom will Jesus Christ and His judges rule over at the advent of the thousand years – punishable by death. And the answer would be all the Christians that ignored the call to be discipled to Christlikeness, or perfection, at the advent and during the seven years leading into the final three-and-a-half year tribulation period. And that is where the mystery of Revelation is unveiled, in that the words of Revelation is aimed at the Church and the two woman representing the sanctuary of God. The one woman pure in her pursuit and relationship with God the Father as her Husband through Jesus Christ in the power of the Holy Spirit. The other woman increasingly given to the idols and pursuit of men, becoming estranged from her relationship with God the Father. Yes we see many, many, many innocent non-Christian bystanders affected by the circumstances in the seven year lead-up period. One example is that one third of the human race is erased by smoke, sulphur and fire surely including Christian and non-Christian alike. But ultimately Revelation is about the destruction of the woman turned harlot, her off-spring, the system she idolised, the persons given to her sanctuary and everything their works represented and created. Once removed the Nations will have a true representation of God the Father, and stand a chance to be redeemed.

Finally we get to the issue of a rapture. Imagine as per our previous salt and pepper analogy that you look up and you can see Jesus Christ return. On His way down all current and historical Christians are taken-up into the sky and then disappear with Jesus Christ on His way back to heaven. Then after off-loading them all in heaven, He again returns to earth with 144 000 men to rule for a thousand years. It seems a bit chaotic doesn't it – all the coming down and going up again? Perhaps starting from the back it is easier to place a mind-map for ourselves. God the Father right at the end will have His judgement day following Jesus' millennium rule. Here, every single person that ever walked the earth will have to rise from their grave and appear before God the Father, each receiving their judgement namely: a second death in the fires of hell or life eternal. The only crowd that will not be subject to this day is the select group that will join Jesus Christ as He returns for a second time to earth, this time to stay and rule for one-thousand years. Any other picture sets us up for confusion and a very busy highway with traffic to-and-fro during the Revelation period –

don't you think?

Surprisingly after a thousand years where Christ accurately represents the kingdom of God, we are surprised to learn that Satan is allowed on more purpose before he becomes the third ever thrown into hell. Satan is released and somehow finds it possible to deceive Nations and a great multitude of people on the earth after they have been and have seen a thousand years of discipleship under Jesus Christ. Our only solace is probably in what is not mentioned is that millions must have been salvaged under the accurate rule of Jesus Christ. But sadly still there is one final major rebellion against Jesus Christ, His camp and the beloved city which we can assume to be Jerusalem.

Here the mercy of God the Father ends for people to redeem themselves through Jesus Christ to Him. The Father Himself appears to crush this rebellion, and heaven and earth is rolled up – in the eight thousandth year since Adam and Eve walked the earth. We see everyone appearing before God's throne for judgement. And notably death and hades become only the fourth to be cast into the burning fires of hell. Those not found in the scroll of life that was handed to Jesus Christ is then judged to receive the second death and cast into the everlasting burning fire of hell.

Chapter 21 and 22: This chapter is so beautiful that it nearly does not warrant any commentary. Except perhaps that we sketch for ourselves the true painting of what God the Father intended for it to be... before the deception and harlotry commenced. We here see that it is God the Father that sits enthroned in heaven. The sanctuary of God itself is now with men and no longer represented by a woman, and He is amongst us. Our righteous works adorn the new city Jerusalem, which comes down and is given as city to Jesus Christ as bride. With that God the Father will never be mis-represented again and we stand to benefit from it as His sons and daughters. It ends a cycle of near seven thousand years of human history intermingled with Spiritual history where first with Adam and Eve, then with

Israel, then Israel and Judah and then during the Church era the woman as representative of the true heavenly sanctuary of God, because of idolatry, pursued material things of men as opposed to Spiritual things in relationship with the Father. With that the world paid dearly for it.

The book of Revelation ends where you see this Tree of Life again that was first shown in Genesis chapter 2. It shows its roots by the living waters – the Holy Spirit. With Jesus Christ the root of David as the trunk of the tree. And its branches delivering twelve kinds of fruit and leaves causing healing to the Nations. Nations you might ask? Yes there are even in the New Heaven and the New Earth different trees again consisting of different Nations. And then there is the Tree of Life with its fruits and leaves accessible for the Nations.

18 THE BEGINNING
OR THE END?

"Surely the Lord God does nothing,
Unless He reveals His secret to His
servants the prophets"" Amos 3: 7

If you have gotten this far with this book whilst simultaneously gaining the ability to read the book of Revelation in one sitting – well done. Certainly working through Revelation we experience feeling good emotions, but also feelings of lamentation in your soul as we ask ourselves what the central theme of the book of Revelation is? The answer would hopefully always be that it is God the Father's desire, or you could say His will, that each Christian in each Church should grow to a perfected Saint – in other words achieve Christlikeness in their maturity. If that remains the central theme in our study of the book of Revelation... we are on a virtuous track!

This theme of the correct discipleship path already commences with the author John that achieved a state of open "eyes" at the end of the book of John after three-and-a-half years of discipleship under Christ Jesus.

We then considered that our forward look can be likened to us standing on a timeline looking frontward into the future and perceiving a pepper shaker followed by a salt shaker coming down from heaven. However, even with the pepper shaker representing deceit sent into the Church, we note that there is a seven year preparation period in the Church to prepare Christians in the discipleship path of righteousness. And that it is only Christians that is not prepared to repent and follow in this way of righteousness that is overcome by the deceit sent by God into the Church.

The pure Church/es manages to grow 144 000 male offspring prior to the commencement of a three-and-a-half year period where deception will be the order of the day. This deception will emulate the Kingdom of God and will be represented by the number 6-6-6 which is a number of men in the flesh. As church going men and woman are indoctrinated in soul, heart and mind into this system during the tribulation period they will receive the spiritual mark of 6-6-6 on their forehead and right hand. The number will represent a unified kingdom of Nations of men with Satan on the throne of this kingdom. Also the false Church of men that works in communion with the unified kingdom. And from the "children", men and woman, born from this communion a central city emerges from where the anti-Christ will rule. This all in contrast to God the Father seated on the throne of the Kingdom of heaven, led by the Spirit of God. And a spiritual Church in communion with the Kingdom of God from which the "children", men and woman, born in Spirit create a city with their words and actions from where Jesus Christ will rule.

The central theme of Revelation therefore remains the discipleship path on how we produce "kingly wine" that once pressed produces wine that smells and tastes appetizing to God the Father. Christlike individuals perfected in love. The equilibrium in the daily lives of these individuals in the Christian community consisting of a balance between sacrifice and offering. With sacrifice being daily individual communion with God the Father to walk in purity and holiness with their bodies, eyes and ears. And daily thanksgiving with their mouth and tongue glorifying and honouring God, whilst at the same time honouring brothers and sister in their community and men in general in society. That equally balance by serving diligently in their Christian community.

In summary then the Book of Revelation is all about the closing of the Church age heralding in the one thousand year rule of Jesus Christ and ultimately ending with God's judgement day. At that time the old heaven and earth removed and replaced by a new heaven and earth. It turns out that by Churches engrafting individual believers onto the Tree of Life and seeing to it that they bear Spiritual fruit were the only woman or sanctuary or Church accurately representing the sanctuary of God the Father. During the return of Jesus Christ the false Church, dominant Nations, and Satan is captured and either thrown into hell or bound for Christ's rule. With the Spiritual Tree of Life always embedded on God's land, encompassing the entire Promised Land given to Israel when they entered the land from Egypt. Jesus Christ and elected Christians rule with an "iron fist" as this Tree of Life grows to cover the entire earth with shade for the Nations and a resting place for all the birds from heaven. For the first time since Adam and Eve, Israel in the Old Testament and during the Church era we then see that the sanctuary of God in heaven is accurately represented here on the Earth during Jesus Christ's rule.

The book of Revelation does not signify prophecies of the end... but rather prophecies of a new beginning. Yes the curtain on the era or Church dispensation is drawing to a close. However not before the a heightened period in this dispensation where the pure Church masters the discipleship path to birth and raise perfected Saints. This will herald in a new beginning where Jesus Christ Himself will rule during a new dispensation here on the earth to herald in the return of God the Father. This will replace everything we currently know and think on how to manage and rule government, business, economy, finances, relationships, worship, and sacrifice and offering. However to birth this new beginning here on the earth all humans and creation itself have to face and herald in the day of the Lord – which according to all Old Testament prophecy is not something to look forward to but a frightening prospect. Therefore the message of Revelation is as sweet as honey in our mouth when we initially contemplate the message in celebration. But the impact of the day of the Lord on society and especially in the Church as we know our brothers and sisters is indeed something to cause lamentation in our souls and indeed bitter in our stomach. Come Jesus Christ, as we pray for the souls, hearts, minds and strength of all Christians to return to God the Father, Amen.

When we prophesy... we prophesy only in part. I am certain as you spend quality time with God the Father that He will give you different dreams, visions and interpretations from another angle to that written in this book. Even as I close there is more that I can add or aspects I could change as each day brings more insights that better represent what lies ahead of us. But that you can add or work out on your own time. The important part is that you grow in your personal relationship with God the Father, through Jesus Christ in the power and truth of the Holy Spirit. And if this book contributed in motivating you towards that personal goal it has accomplished what I set out to do. Enjoy working through not only Revelation but for that matter the entire Bible and growing in personal relationship with God.

BIBLIOGRAPHY / REFERENCES

B.R. Hicks. *Growing Up to the Fullness of Eternal Life*. Christ Gospel Bible Institute.

B. Sorge. *Pain Perplexity and Promotion – A Prophetic Interpretation of the Book of Job*. Grandview: Oasis House Publishers, 2009.

http://atheism.about.com/library/FAQs/christian/blchron_xian_inquisition.htm

http://ngm.nationalgeographic.com/2011/07/food-ark/food-variety-graphic

http://upload.wikimedia.org/wikipedia/commons/b/b2/Comparison_gender_life_expectancy_CIA_factbook.svg

http://www.YouTube.com/David Pawson: Galatians (Unlocking The Bible Series)

http://www.YouTube.com/David Pawson: Romans Part 1 (Unlocking The Bible Series)

https://www.ec.gc.ca/inre-nwri/default.asp?lang=En&n=235D11EB-1

http://www.jewfaq.org/m/holidaya.htm

http://www.thedailybeast.com/articles/2010/01/15/historys-10-worst-earthquakes.html

http://www.YouTube.com/Louie Giglio: Indescribable

http://www.YouTube.com/Meteorite Explosion Part 2 – Russia Chelyabinsk2/15/2013

http://www.YouTube.com/The great revelation 12 signs in the Heavens – The revisited & revealed

http://www.youtube.com/watch?v=wkQuU2hRLLA

J. David Pawson. *Unlocking the Bible*. London: Harper Collins Publishers, 2007.

Joyce Meyer. *Battlefield of the mind*. Nashville, Tennessee: Faith Words Publishers, a division of the Hachette Book Group, 2011.

"Report of the National Intelligence Council's 2020 Project", *Mapping the Global Future*, 2004 (http:\\bookstore.gpo.gov; GPO Stock 041-015-0024-6; ISBN 0-16-073-218-2.)

R. Foster. *Celebration of Discipline – The path to Spiritual Growth*. London: Hodder & Stoughton LTD, 1989.

9 780620 642705